COLORADO ALPINE TRAIL RUNS

ANNALISE GRUETER

The Colorado Mountain Club Press
Golden, Colorado

Colorado Alpine Trail Runs
© 2022 Annalise Grueter

All rights reserved. No part of this publication may be reproduced or transmitted in any form or by any means, electronic or mechanical, including photocopy, recording, or by any information storage and retrieval system without permission in writing from the publisher.

Published by The Colorado Mountain Club Press
710 10th Street, Suite 200, Golden, CO 80401
303-996-2743 | cmcpress@cmc.org | cmcpress.org

Founded in 1912, The Colorado Mountain Club is the largest outdoor recreation, education, and conservation organization in the Rocky Mountains. Look for our books at your local bookstore or outdoor retailer, or online at cmcpress.org.

Corrections: We greatly appreciate when readers alert us to errors or outdated information by emailing cmcpress@cmc.org.

Annalise Grueter: photographer, unless otherwise noted
Vicki Hopewell: design and composition
Sarah Gorecki: publisher

Cover photo: Moss campion on the trail to Electric Pass Peak and Leahy Peak.

Distributed to the book trade by:
Mountaineers Books
1001 SW Klickitat Way, Suite 201, Seattle, WA 98134
800-553-4453 | mountaineersbooks.org

We gratefully acknowledge the financial support of the people of Colorado through the Scientific and Cultural Facilities District of greater metropolitan Denver for our publishing activities.

TOPOGRAPHIC MAPS created with CalTopo software.

Printed in the United States of America

ISBN 978-1-937052-76-8

22 23 24 / 10 9 8 7 6 5 4 3 2 1

This guidebook is dedicated to my father, whose passion for the outdoors was instilled in me at an early age, and whose memory I feel especially close to in these high places. It is also dedicated to my high school cross-country running and skiing coaches, who first introduced me to alpine trail running and the particular kind of beauty found at and above tree line.

A runner descends foggy
West Maroon Pass on
the Four Pass Loop.
Photo by Madeline Fones

CONTENTS

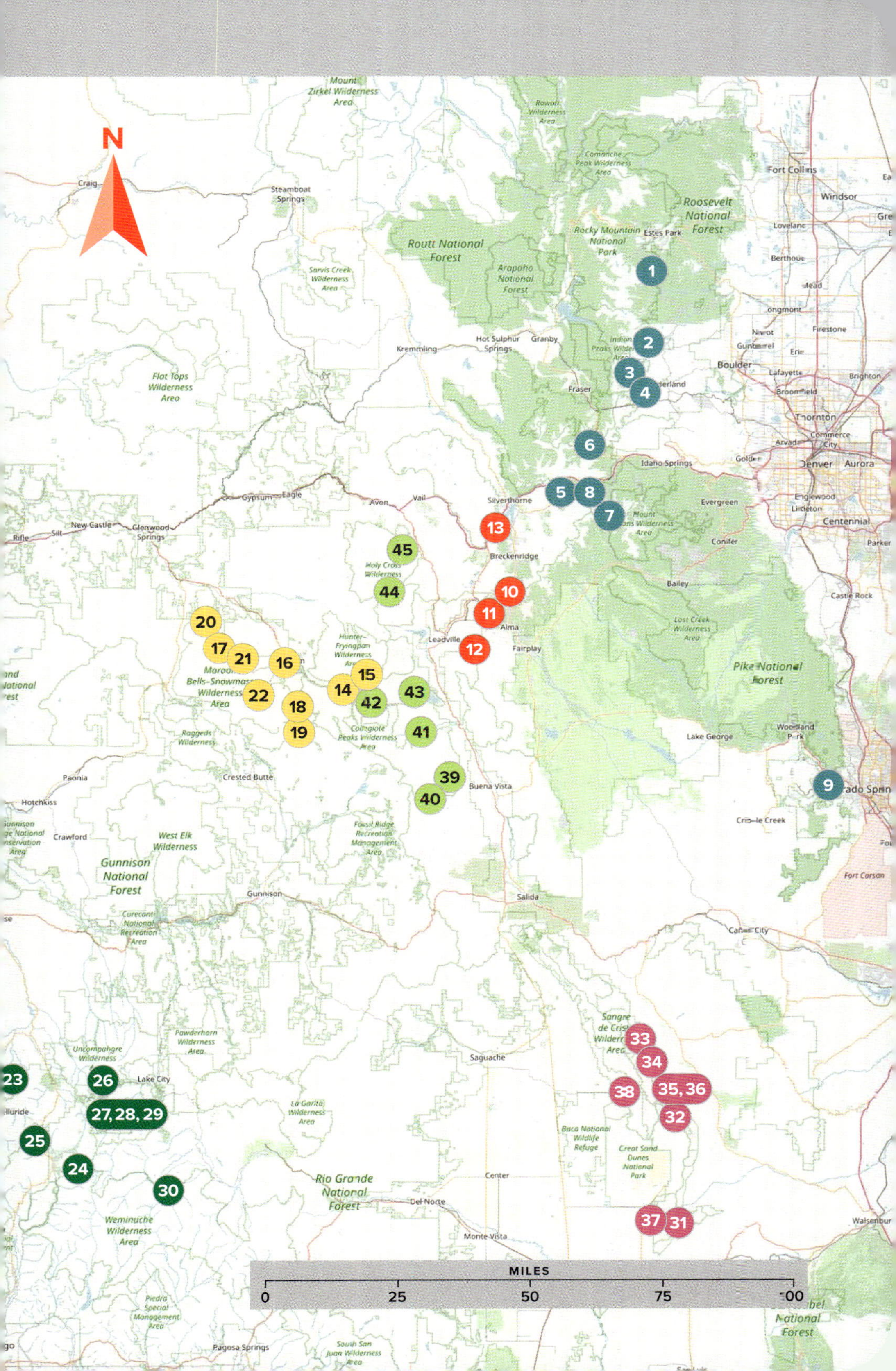

N
Craig
Steamboat Springs
Mount Zirkel Wilderness Area
Sarvis Creek Wilderness Area
Rawah Wilderness Area
Fort Collins
Windsor
Loveland
Roosevelt National Forest
Comanche Peak Wilderness Area
Routt National Forest
Rocky Mountain National Park
Estes Park
Longmont
Berthoud
Firestone
Flat Tops Wilderness Area
Kremmling
Hot Sulphur Springs
Granby
Indian Peaks Wilderness Area
Fraser
Arapaho National Forest
Nederland
Boulder
Lafayette
Gunbarrel
Erie
Brighton
Broomfield
Thornton
Gypsum
Eagle
Avon
Vail
Silverthorne
Idaho Springs
Golden
Denver
Aurora
Commerce City
Glenwood Springs
New Castle
Rifle
Silt
Breckenridge
Mount Evans Wilderness Area
Evergreen
Englewood
Littleton
Centennial
Holy Cross Wilderness
Leadville
Alma
Fairplay
Conifer
Bailey
Castle Rock
Hunter–Fryingpan Wilderness Area
Maroon Bells-Snowmass Wilderness Area
Lost Creek Wilderness Area
Pike National Forest
Raggeds Wilderness
Collegiate Peaks Wilderness Area
Lake George
Woodland Park
Paonia
Crested Butte
Buena Vista
Colorado Springs
Cripple Creek
Hotchkiss
Fossil Ridge Recreation Management Area
Crawford
West Elk Wilderness
Fort Carson
Gunnison National Forest
Gunnison
Salida
Curecanti National Recreation Area
Cañon City
Powderhorn Wilderness Area
Saguache
Sangre de Cristo Wilderness Area
Uncompahgre Wilderness
Lake City
La Garita Wilderness Area
Baca National Wildlife Refuge
Great Sand Dunes National Park
Telluride
Center
Rio Grande National Forest
Del Norte
Walsenburg
Weminuche Wilderness Area
Monte Vista
Piedra Special Management Area
Pagosa Springs
South San Juan Wilderness Area
San Luis
National Forest
MILES
0   25   50   75   100

INTRODUCTION
A Background on Trail and Mountain Running

Running on trails is a fun, high-energy activity that has been steadily gaining popularity for decades. But what is trail running, exactly? The term "trail running" is actually a catchall phrase for a few different, unique sports, including trail running, mountain running, and skyrunning.

Traditional trail running, by its purest definition, is a form of running and jogging usually done on designated hiking trails. While it may well include running on rolling terrain, it does not require intense amounts of steep vertical gain or much routefinding. Mountain running, a popular recreational sport in Europe that has been gaining popularity across North America, is defined as running, jogging, and walking on trails or roads in mountainous terrain with *significant* amounts of vertical gain. Uphill and downhill slopes vary between 5 degrees and 20 degrees, but despite that steepness, mountain running routes generally avoid dangerous terrain.

Skyrunning, meanwhile, is a category of mountain running where routes have a minimum average slope grade of 6 degrees and a required portion of every route

The Phantom Terrace Loop is an excellent intermediate example of Colorado skyrunning.

with a slope of 30 degrees or more. In skyrunning competitions, vertical gain for routes meets or exceeds 6,600 feet, and competitors may use spikes, crampons, or poles for aid in addition to their hands. Iconic skyrunning, whether on or off maintained trail, is on terrain that is either on the crest of exposed alpine ridges or traverses across extreme side slopes. Highly popular in central Europe, skyrunning is growing in popularity in the United States, with several races annually across the American West.

In this guidebook, the vast majority of routes fall within the definition of mountain running in that they are largely on maintained trails, at significant altitudes, with minimal, if any, sections of dangerous or exposed terrain. Routes rated as Black Diamond and Double Black Diamond (defined under *Difficulty* on p. 4) are rated as such because they fall within the more extreme definition of skyrunning, including routes off of maintained trail and that may include exposed ridge crests and scrambling. Some optional add-ons to Green or Blue routes are more difficult than the routes to which these add-ons connect.

Alpine trail running comes with risks beyond that of lower-elevation trail running. These risks include altitude sickness, more variable temperatures, exposure to changeable weather, and more challenging navigation. Guidance for managing these risks is detailed in the *How to Use This Guide* section that follows and elaborated upon with more detail within specific route descriptions.

When risks are adequately managed, alpine trail running also leads to truly spectacular views, uniquely sublime outdoor adventures, and opportunities for gorgeous photos and self-guided experiential education that few other outdoor activities facilitate.

Happy trails!

HOW TO USE THIS GUIDE

This guide features forty-five spectacular trails from around Colorado, organized by mountain range. Each route description includes data about the run, trailhead directions, a thorough description of the trail, and how to navigate the route. Runs are presented in an order based primarily on their location within each region. The routes are listed with consideration for technical progression as well as a logical driving order should readers choose to tackle an entire range's worth of runs in a single trip.

Routes are listed starting with nine in the Front Range, then four highlights from Summit County and surrounding towns, nine in the running mecca of the Elk Mountains, eight each for the San Juan and Sangre de Cristo Ranges, and finishing with seven in the Sawatch Range. Section maps and an overall map highlight the numbered routes for quick reference. To further help you decide on a route, the back of the guide offers handy at-a-glance checklists of the routes listed by mileage and vertical gain.

DATA SECTION AND OTHER ROUTE DETAILS

The data reference section for each route compiles basic information such as starting elevation, highest elevation, total elevation gain, estimated run time, nearest town, and more. Other details are included in the route descriptions as relevant. Let's take a closer look at those categories and details.

Total Distance

Total distance is provided for each route in miles, followed by an indication of whether the route is a loop, an out-and-back, or a point-to-point run. Distances are calculated using Global Positioning System (GPS) technology and topographic mapping programs; however, note that total mileages can vary by small amounts. When a route offers an optional extension or variation (an "add-on"), that additional mileage and vertical gain will be described in the route description but will not be included in the listed total distance, as these extensions are optional.

Starting Elevation and High Point Elevation

Starting point elevation and a route's high point/summit elevation are provided for every route. This allows runners to better evaluate each route based on their own abilities and interests. If you are new to trail running, it is recommended to start with the shortest, easiest routes in each range and work your way up to the harder and higher elevation routes.

Total Elevation Gain

Total elevation gain is an additional tool to evaluate the difficulty of a route. Generally speaking, routes with less than 700 feet of vertical gain per mile are easier, while those with more than 1,000 feet of vertical gain are difficult and likely to involve more power hiking than running.

Difficulty/Runability

Routes are designated as Green for Beginner, Blue for Intermediate, Black Diamond for Difficult, and Double Black Diamond for Most Difficult. These ratings represent the author's evaluation of the overall difficulty and runability of each route, accounting for distance, elevation gain, trail quality, highest elevation, and effort level. Note that the Most Difficult routes are either very long or involve exposed, off-trail terrain where a helmet is a good idea.

Round-trip Time

Each route includes an estimated round-trip time range. These estimates are based on the author's personal experiences on the routes as well as recorded times from various athletes. Given the high elevation of the routes, many steeper uphill times are based on a 20- to 30-minute-mile pace. It is certainly possible to run, jog, and hike the routes faster or slower than the estimated times. If you are not sure of your running pace at elevation compared to your home elevation, plan your excursion based on the long end of the time range.

Your level of fitness, comfort with technical running, acclimatization to altitude, and day-of conditions will significantly affect your time. Starting on shorter, easier routes after establishing a trail running base at lower elevations will help set you up for success and measure where you fall within the estimated times.

Best Time of Year to Run

Given that the average starting elevation of most of these runs is slightly over 10,000 feet, very few of them can be run year-round. For the majority of routes, the best time to run will be between mid-June and mid-October. If the best timing for a particular route falls outside of those general parameters, it will be noted within the route description.

Alpine trails become considerably higher risk with snow, so note that many of the routes in this book will be impassable in winter and spring. Routes in this guidebook that are possible in snowy conditions with a clear forecast include Mount Sniktau, Quandary Peak, Aspen Highlands, Chasm Lake, and Mount Bierstadt. If you choose to undertake an alpine run in snowy conditions, it is recommended that you carry ample additional layers and additional emergency gear, and that you check the avalanche forecast as soon as possible beforehand.

Water Points

The majority of routes do not have potable water available at the trailhead, so come prepared. Some routes have creeks or streams for filtering; others do not. It is always recommended that runners carry a form of water treatment and have at least one liter of extra water at the trailhead/in their vehicle for after a run. If a useful water point exists on a route, it will be noted in the route description.

Parking/Permits

Road access and parking situations vary per route. Whether trailheads are accessed by paved or dirt roads, 2WD or 4WD, and whether permits or fees are required are noted in a route's *Getting There* section.

Nearest Town

The nearest town is provided for each route to assist with orientation and planning. When a trailhead is roughly halfway between two towns, both towns are listed and the distance to each are mentioned in the route's *Getting There* section.

Add-ons

Some routes are near other points of interest, such as nearby lakes or peaks. A few routes also have alternative navigation options for part of the run. When this is the case, an add-on (or alternative) will be noted in the data block, a description will be included in the route details, and the add-on route will be shown in green on the map.

Bikes and Dogs

For the extra-enthusiastic athletes out there, it is possible to bike to some trailheads rather than drive. Where applicable, this information will be included in the *Getting There* section of a route description, including guidance for where to lock a bike.

Some runners enjoy bringing their dog(s) along on runs for company. It is generally encouraged to keep dogs on leash on public land, even when not required. If dogs are allowed on a trail, it will be noted within a route's description.

LEAVE NO TRACE AND TRAIL GUIDELINES

Leave No Trace principles establish guidelines for responsible outdoor practice. The seven rules follow, along with recommendations for application in the context of trail and mountain running.

Plan Ahead and Prepare

Alpine running is a significant undertaking—prepare for it. Read the route description in this book in order to set expectations, check the weather forecast as close to the run as you can, pack thoughtfully for your expected run time and the anticipated conditions, and plan for your drive time to the trailhead. Have a backup plan and make sure someone knows where you are going and when they can expect you to check in afterward.

Travel and Camp on Durable Surfaces

No matter where you run, thoughtful travel is important. For runs on maintained trail, make sure to stay on trail and refrain from disturbing your surroundings. For routes or sections of routes that are not on maintained trail, be intentional about leaving as little impact as possible, treading on rock or more durable terrain as much as possible, and avoiding fragile alpine flora.

Dispose of Waste Properly

Everyone deserves the same pristine experience that you are seeking. Be sure to pack out all wrappers and food (including fruit peels or cores; although natural, in the arid alpine spaces of Colorado, they decompose very slowly and disrupt the ecosystem); keep track of all your belongings; and if you need to take a bathroom break during your run, make sure to pack out any paper (an empty zip-top bag in your pack comes in handy) and dig a proper cathole if needed (at least six inches deep, below tree line if possible). You may also choose to carry a wag bag, which is a sanitary way to pack out your solid waste, and can be purchased at outdoor stores.

Leave What You Find

Tempting as it might be, do not take anything other than photos. Leave unique pebbles, interesting twigs, and beautiful wildflowers where they are. Part of the magic

Comanche Peak is an optional addition to the Phantom Terrace Loop, and the summit offers stunning southern views.

of these places is the effort it takes to visit them, and everyone deserves to enjoy that same, exclusive view if they make the trek to do so.

Minimize (Campfire) Impacts

If you are including camping in your run adventures, be sure to minimize your impacts. For those who may be camping or fastpacking multiple days on a single trail, it is recommended to limit fire to a lightweight camp stove and a lighter. Only use these on flat surfaces away from foliage, preferably on a flat stretch of rock.

Respect Wildlife

Smaller wildlife will likely be scarce, as your size and motion tend to scare them away before you can get close. If you do encounter wildlife at close quarters, take only pictures; do not disturb, harass, or feed them. For larger wildlife, such as mountain goats, bighorn sheep, bears, or moose, give them a wide berth and backtrack if necessary (particularly in the case of moose and bears). Avoid coming between a mother and her young, as this will provoke a defensive response and put both you and the wildlife in danger. If you are running with a dog, keep them on leash.

Be Considerate of Other Visitors

When passing hikers on trails, make sure to give them ample notice and be polite and friendly. While many are happy to give right-of-way to the fastest-moving party, others will expect you to cede right-of-way to them. If you choose to listen to music on your runs, use headphones or earbuds rather than speakers, but not at a volume that prevents you from hearing any communication from other trail users.

TEN ESSENTIALS

This list is based on the essential survival items recommended for outdoor recreation in case of emergency. These essentials have been included in *Mountaineering: The Freedom of the Hills* since 1974 and are recommended by most outdoor organizations, including the Colorado Mountain Club. I have included specific guidance for alpine running in each of the following categories.

1. Navigation

While this book provides guidelines and directions for each route, it is valuable insurance to also have a map with you during each run. To keep navigation fast and easily accessible, map out a GPX track on your phone or watch; if using your phone, it works well to keep it in one of the front pockets of your running pack. For many of the routes, you can find GPX tracks available for download on a number of websites (often categorized for hiking). Alternately, you can use a mapping site like caltopo.com to manually copy the routes as pictured in this guidebook and then save the GPX track to your watch or phone. Study the routes in detail beforehand to make sure you know the major intersections to stay on track. You can also use your phone camera to take photos of route descriptions before your run to have them available for reference mid-run.

2. Illumination

Many of these routes are appropriate to start before sunrise. It is also good practice to carry a headlamp when travelling in the backcountry. For all runs, be sure to bring a headlamp with fresh batteries. If starting before dawn, it is appropriate to wear the headlamp; otherwise, store it in a secure pocket of your running pack.

3. Sun Protection

In addition to applying sunscreen to exposed skin, many runners choose to wear lightweight, long-sleeved sun shirts and light, brimmed running hats. For a long run, you may want to carry a small tube of extra sunscreen to reapply periodically. Nose, cheeks, and exposed shoulders and back are particularly vulnerable at elevation.

4. First Aid

For shorter runs, carrying a small amount of ibuprofen and a few Band-Aids is always a good idea. For longer runs or if you are injury-prone, be sure to include a small roll of gauze, a roll of sports tape (to be used with gauze for cuts and abrasions), a small roll of athletic tape (for strained fascia), and a bit of topical pain reliever for achy joints or muscles. If you tend to develop blisters when you run, bring a small blister kit.

5. Tools

Several of the routes in this book take 4–6 hours or more. In addition to a headlamp and extra batteries, other tools that come in handy on a long run include a small amount of paracord, a lightweight multi-tool, and a bandanna, all of which are wonderfully versatile should you need to make repairs to your running pack or other gear en route.

6. Fire

In the case of long runs, this category is covered by the *Insulation* and *Emergency Shelter* sections. Generally, the recommendation for use of fire is for warmth when camping below tree line. As fires are discouraged, if not banned, above tree line in Colorado due to the delicate ecosystems, warmth can be ensured with insulative clothing layers and emergency shelter.

7. Emergency Shelter

For shorter runs, shelter can be covered by items listed under *Insulation*. For longer runs, you may also want to carry a lightweight space blanket or emergency bivvy. While it is unlikely these will be necessary, especially if you check the weather forecast before committing to a run (which is highly recommended), they are a small amount of extra weight for added safety.

8. Nutrition

Long, hard runs burn a lot of energy. Be sure to bring 200–300 calories per anticipated hour of your run, plus an additional 300–500 calories just in case. A mix of carbs, protein, and a little fat is ideal for shorter runs and absolutely essential for longer runs—so essential, in fact, that you'll find even more details and recommendations in the *Safety, Gear, and Fueling* section that follows.

9. Hydration

What you require will vary depending on your weight, length/difficulty of your run, and temperatures, but a reasonable approximation is 500–600 mL per anticipated hour of your run. Some runners use soft bottles, stored in pockets up front for easy access, while others use water bladders that fit into a sleeve in the back of a running pack with a small hose for sipping. Some form of water treatment is also essential for longer runs, whether you prefer a UV light, lightweight filter, or chemical mixture. For more information, see *Safety, Gear, and Fueling*.

10. Insulation

Weather can change rapidly above tree line, and even the warmest temperatures are cooler compared to towns and cities. Often, altitudes of 13,000 or 14,000 feet can have close to freezing temperatures with windchill even on a summer day. Wearing (or packing) adequate insulative layers is crucial. A wind jacket is the key piece of insulation for high elevations, well accompanied by a headband or hat and light gloves. A neck buff is also nice for cold mornings or breezy days. An extra pair of light wool socks also can help.

SAFETY, GEAR, AND FUELING

While safer than many other outdoor pursuits (such as climbing and mountaineering), alpine running is not without risk and exposes you to more risk than trail running below tree line. This section outlines two of the most significant risks—altitude sickness and alpine weather—and provides guidance for self-care in terms of appropriate gear, fueling, and hydration.

Altitude and Potential Risks

Altitude sickness is a possibility and a danger at high elevations. While it can occur below 8,000 feet, it typically occurs above that elevation. Every route described in this book exceeds 11,000 feet, and several routes have high points between 13,000 feet and 14,000 feet. A third of the routes go above 14,000 feet. Only one run (Pikes Peak, p. 47) starts below 8,000 feet, but even that route tops out above 14,000 feet. In sum, altitude sickness is a concern for alpine runners interested in these routes.

Acute mountain sickness (AMS) and more severe forms of altitude sickness become more likely if you are improperly acclimated, dehydrated, sunburnt, or have not ingested adequate calories and a balance of electrolytes. The best way to prevent altitude sickness is to gradually increase the altitude at which you are exerting yourself. If you normally run at sea level or below the elevation of Denver, Colorado (5,280 feet), start by becoming comfortable with trail runs at your elevation, then at the elevations of cities such as Boulder (5,318 feet), Golden (5,675 feet), or other Colorado Front Range towns that sit around 5,000 feet in elevation. From there, consider seeking out trail runs that are above 5,000 feet but that remain mostly below tree line. Peter N. Jones's book *The Best Front Range Trail Runs* outlines several such options. Once the 7,000- to 10,000-foot elevations become comfortable, start with the shortest mileage and lowest elevation routes in this guidebook before progressing to higher and longer mileage routes.

Exploring the add-ons to Highland Mary Lakes brings encounters with wildflowers and breathtaking views of the Needles Range.

Symptoms of altitude sickness include shortness of breath, headache, nausea, and a feeling of heaviness in the limbs. These mild symptoms can be treated on the trail with hydration (both water and electrolytes), caffeine, ibuprofen, and quick calories. The most effective treatment, however, is descending in elevation. If you do choose to continue your ascent and your symptoms progress to vomiting, dizziness, severe headache, or the sensation of being drunk, it is important that you descend as soon and as quickly as is safely possible, then gradually hydrate and consume electrolytes. When dehydrated, it can be tempting to drink liquids and ingest salts rapidly, but it is easy to exceed your needs and exacerbate the situation. If you are suffering from altitude sickness or dehydration, take in small amounts of liquid and electrolytes at regular intervals until you begin feeling better, rather than ingest a large amount all at once.

If you experience more severe symptoms than these outlined, such as a blinding headache, wheezing, wet coughing, or racing heart rate, even after descending and resting, seek medical attention as soon as possible, as these can be signs of severe, life-threatening forms of altitude sickness: high-altitude cerebral edema (HACE) or high-altitude pulmonary edema (HAPE).

Alpine Weather

Weather changes quickly above tree line, particularly in high summer due to how heat and evaporation patterns create a microclimate for mountains. Dangerous alpine weather includes thunderstorms, cold temperatures and windchill, and high winds. Always check the weather forecast when planning a run, and plan to be back below tree line before any forecast thunderstorms. Carefully consider the gear you pack based on the temperature and wind forecasts.

It can be helpful to learn how to recognize a variety of cloud types as well, in order to better understand developing weather while you are on a run. Thin, wispy stratus clouds are usually not cause for concern, whereas rapidly growing puffy cumulus clouds are a harbinger of coming monsoon thunderstorms. If you observe the latter on a run, plan to get back below tree line quickly. During July and August, it is possible for a sky to shift from cloudless blue to small fluffy cumulus to heavy and dangerous cumulonimbus clouds in less than an hour. In Colorado, it is typical for summer storms to develop in the southwestern sky and progress north and eastward through the day. It's always a good idea to keep one eye on the trail and one on the sky.

Gear

Although there is overlap between the gear needed for lower-elevation trail running and alpine running, there are some distinct differences. The increased exertion and risk that comes with running above tree line makes some items crucial for alpine running. The guidance in this section is essential.

Running Pack

Given the elevation of these routes, you will want to hydrate even during shorter-mileage runs. On longer-mileage runs, you'll also want snacks. To carry items such as snacks, hydration, and additional layers, a running pack is extremely useful. Running-style packs are smaller and more fitted than typical hiking backpacks; look for one that is 5–10 liters. While some runners use fanny packs, they tend to shift after several miles on rocky trails and so are not highly recommended. A good selection of running packs can be found at your local outdoor store, running store, or online.

Shoes

While there are a huge variety of choices available to trail runners, the key is to choose shoes that are comfortable for your feet. For some, this means thickly cushioned soles, while others may prefer a minimalist style. Consider visiting a running or outdoor store to try on shoes, as these stores tend to offer a wide selection, as well as advice on fit. Stick with a style similar to what you already run in. Grippy tread and a protective rubber toe guard are particularly useful for rocky terrain.

Socks

Cotton socks are a big no-no in the alpine, as they get wet and stay wet, causing discomfort and often blisters. Opt instead for quick-drying Merino wool or midweight synthetic socks. For longer runs (13+ miles), rainy weather, or routes with creek crossings, consider packing an extra pair to switch into.

Wind Jackets/Layers

Since some alpine runs start below tree line and work their way up in elevation, layers are essential. There can be wide temperature differences between trailheads and high points, so don't be fooled by sunny skies, low winds, and cool temps at the start. Key items to bring include a neck gaiter, headband, hat, light gloves, and a lightweight, water-resistant wind jacket.

Fueling and Hydration

As mentioned in *Ten Essentials*, you will want to bring 200–300 calories per anticipated hour of your run, plus an additional 300–500 calories just in case the run goes longer than planned. A mix of carbs, protein, and a little fat is ideal for shorter runs, and for longer runs it is essential. Many runners enjoy gels, gummies, cheese sticks, potato chips or crackers, nuts and nut butter, baby food purees, or a carb- and/or protein-loaded sports drink mix for their water.

Hydration will vary depending on your weight and how much you sweat, but a good approximation is 500–600 mL per anticipated hour of your run. A form of water treatment is also essential for longer runs, whether you prefer a UV light, lightweight filter, or chemical mixture like Aquamira. Outdoor stores carry a variety of lightweight water treatments that are easy to use. The other crucial piece of hydration is appropriate electrolytes, which also depend on your weight and how much you sweat. Test out electrolyte mixes on lower-elevation trail runs to make sure they agree with your stomach, and when you find one you like, carry a backup portion with you on any given run just in case the day is hotter than anticipated.

RUNS AT A GLANCE

FRONT RANGE

		MILEAGE	DIFFICULTY	VERTICAL GAIN	STARTING ELEVATION	HIGH POINT	ADD-ON
1	Chasm Lake	8 mi.	■ Intermediate	2,500'	9,400'	11,800'	no
2	Blue Lake and Mitchell Lake	7 mi.	● Beginner	1,190'	10,350'	11,385'	no
3	Old Baldy	8.5 mi.	■ Intermediate	2,880'	10,160'	13,039'	yes
4	High Lonesome Loop	15.7 mi.	◆ Difficult	3,560'	9,000'	12,020'	no
5	Mount Sniktau	3.8 mi.	● Beginner	1,800'	11,990'	13,234'	yes
6	Mount Flora	6.2 mi.	■ Intermediate	2,275'	11,300'	13,140'	yes
7	Mount Bierstadt	7.5 mi.	■ Intermediate	2,775''	11,500'	14,060'	no
8	Grays and Torreys Peaks	8.5 mi.	■ Intermediate	3,650'	11,250'	14,270'	no
9	Pikes Peak	25.1 mi.	◆◆ Most Difficult	7,545'	6,690'	14,110'	yes

SUMMIT COUNTY

		MILEAGE	DIFFICULTY	VERTICAL GAIN	STARTING ELEVATION	HIGH POINT	ADD-ON
10	Quandary Peak	7 mi.	■ Intermediate	3,450'	10,850'	14,265'	no
11	Decalibron Loop	7.5 mi.	■ Intermediate	3,400'	12,000'	14,286'	no
12	Mount Sherman and Mount Sheridan	6.5 mi.	■ Intermediate	2,750'	12,000'	14,036'	yes
13	Tenmile Traverse	14.7 mi.	◆◆ Most Difficult	8,320'	9,165'	13,633'	yes

ELK RANGE

		MILEAGE	DIFFICULTY	VERTICAL GAIN	STARTING ELEVATION	HIGH POINT	ADD-ON
14	Midway Tarn	4.5 mi.	● Beginner	1,502'	10,512'	11,995'	yes
15	Lost Man Loop	8.8 mi.	■ Intermediate	1,610'	11,510'	12,795'	yes
16	Aspen Highlands	11 mi.	◆ Difficult	4,760'	8,160'	12,360'	yes
17	Capitol Lake	12.6 mi.	■ Intermediate	2,600'	9,463'	11,600'	no
18	Electric Pass Peak and Leahy Peak	12 mi.	■ Intermediate	4,100'	9,880'	13,640'	no
19	Castle Peak	13.5 mi.	◆◆ Most Difficult	4,600'	9,800'	14,260'	yes
20	Mount Sopris	13.5 mi.	◆◆ Most Difficult	4,665'	8,655'	12,966'	yes
21	Snowmass Three Pass Loop	23 mi.	◆◆ Most Difficult	5,930'	8,420'	12,690'	no
22	Four Pass Loop	28 mi.	◆◆ Most Difficult	7,265'	9,576'	12,454'	no

SAN JUAN RANGE

		MILEAGE	DIFFICULTY	VERTICAL GAIN	STARTING ELEVATION	HIGH POINT	ADD-ON
23	Blue Lakes Basin	8.4 mi.	■ Intermediate	2,900'	9,355'	11,760'	yes
24	Highland Mary Lakes	5 mi.	● Beginner	1,340'	10,780'	12,120'	yes
25	Columbine Lake	5.7 mi.	■ Intermediate	2,625'	10,285'	12,720'	no
26	Matterhorn Creek	6.7 mi.	● Beginner	2,465'	10,385'	12,760'	no
27	Handies Peak	8.2 mi.	■ Intermediate	3,650'	10,420'	14,048	yes
28	Cooper Lake	10 mi.	■ Intermediate	2,380'	10,420'	12,800'	no
29	Redcloud Peak	9 mi.	■ Intermediate	3,700'	10,420'	14,034	yes
30	The Window	24.8 mi.	◆◆ Most Difficult	4,900'	9,350'	13,057	no

SANGRE DE CRISTO RANGE

		MILEAGE	DIFFICULTY	VERTICAL GAIN	STARTING ELEVATION	HIGH POINT	ADD-ON
31	Lily Lake	6.8 mi.	● Beginner	1,700'	10,615'	12,310'	no
32	Music Pass	7.2 mi.	● Beginner	2,090'	9,310'	11,400'	yes
33	Lake of the Clouds	10.2 mi.	■ Intermediate	2,190'	9,480'	11,665'	no
34	Phantom Terrace Loop	12.6 mi.	◆ Difficult	4,400'	8,920'	12,850	yes
35	Humboldt Peak	9.8 mi.	◆ Difficult	4,200'	9,950'	14,064	no
36	Obstruction Peak	12.8 mi.	◆◆ Most Difficult	4,700'	9,950'	13,799	no
37	Zapata Lake	9.6 mi.	■ Intermediate	3,300'	9,100'	11,930	no
38	Willow Lake	9.6 mi.	■ Intermediate	3,500'	8,850'	11,765'	no

SAWATCH RANGE

		MILEAGE	DIFFICULTY	VERTICAL GAIN	STARTING ELEVATION	HIGH POINT	ADD-ON
39	Bear Lake	10.7 mi	■ Intermediate	2,700'	9,450'	12,410'	no
40	Mount Yale	9.5 mi.	◆ Difficult	4,330'	9,935'	14,200'	yes
41	Belford and Oxford via Elkhead Pass	11 mi.	◆ Difficult	5,800'	9,650'	14,186	no
42	Igloo Peak	5.1 mi.	● Beginner	1,200'	12,100'	13,060'	yes
43	Mount Elbert	10.7 mi.	◆ Difficult	4,080'	10,510'	14,433'	no
44	Fancy Pass and Missouri Lakes Loop	8.8 mi.	■ Intermediate	2,770'	10,090'	12,310'	no
45	Notch Mountain Shelter	10.4 mi.	◆ Difficult	2,800'	10,380'	13,095'	no

FRONT RANGE

Chasm Lake 1
Blue Lake and Mitchell Lake 2
Old Baldy 3
High Lonesome Loop 4
Mount Flora 6
Mount Sniktau 5
Grays and Torreys Peaks 8
Mount Bierstadt 7
Pikes Peak 9
MILES
0 5 10 15 20 25 30 35 40 45 50 55 60

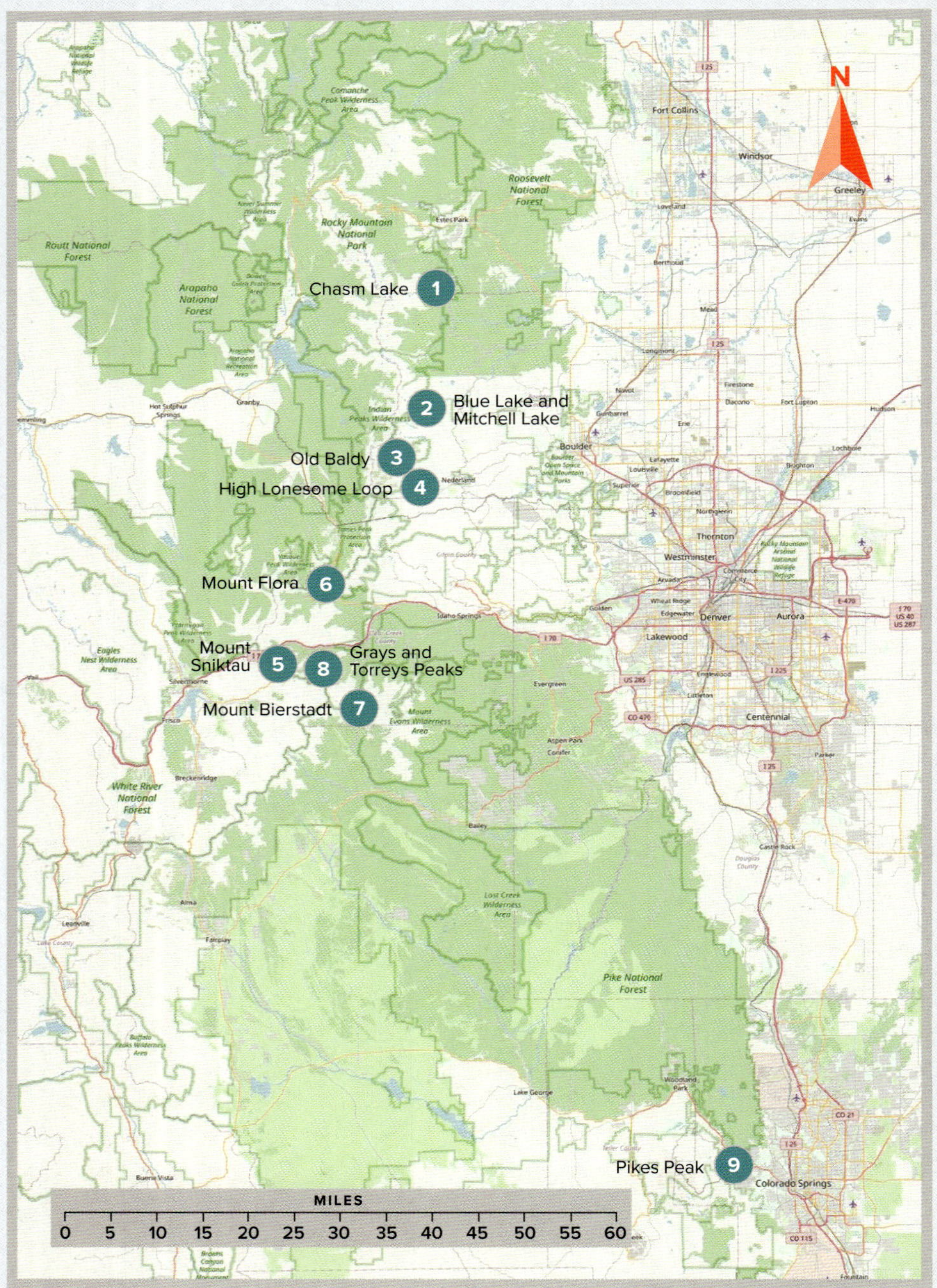

CHASM LAKE

Total Distance	8 miles (out-and-back)
Starting Elevation	9,400 feet
High Point Elevation	11,800 feet
Total Elevation Gain	2,500 feet
Difficulty	■ Intermediate
Round-trip Time	1.25–2.5 hours
Runability	90%
Nearest Town	Estes Park

COMMENT: Longs Peak is one of Colorado's most famous mountains, popular among climbers, mountaineers, painters, photographers, and sightseers. Its looming northeast face, known as the Diamond, features a sheer 1,000-foot drop in the 2,400 feet of prominence between Chasm Lake and the summit. This route's breathtaking view of the Diamond is well worth a visit and inspiring to behold. This route is excellent for acclimation before tackling a higher-elevation run.

The iconic Longs
Peak Diamond

GETTING THERE: Follow CO Highway 7 to Longs Peak Road and drive 1.1 miles to the Longs Peak Ranger Station trailhead, which has a paved lot with an outhouse and is 2WD-accessible. As of 2021, between Memorial Day weekend and mid-October, both a National Parks pass/daily entrance fee and a timed entry permit/reservation are required to enter Rocky Mountain National Park. More details can be found at nps.gov/romo. This trailhead can also be reached by road or mountain bike; duathletes will want to bring a bike lock.

THE ROUTE: Clocking in at 8 miles round-trip, the run to and from Chasm Lake is extremely popular among local trail runners. The trail is very well maintained and the vertical gain gradual, making it an excellent alpine training run as you work up acclimation for 13,000- and 14,000-foot peaks.

The trail winds upward through boreal forest for the first 2.3 miles. The ground underfoot here is soft and forgiving, in places carpeted with needles from the fir, spruce, and iconic lodgepole pine trees populous in much of Colorado. Should you be interested in pausing to identify and distinguish between trees, note that pines have distinctive longer, bunched needles; firs have soft, flat, short needles; and spruces wield the sharpest, stiffest needles.

As you gain elevation, the forest trees become gnarled and decrease in height. Don't be fooled, though; these shorter trees are not necessarily any younger than the taller forest closer to the trailhead. The gnarled wood (called krummholz) is simply an indication of the stunting effect that elevation has on larger flora.

Shortly after leaving tree line, you'll reach a turnoff at 3.4 miles. A turn right (northwest) heads toward the Longs Peak Boulder Field, but you want to head roughly southwest, a path that brings you into the belly of the Chasm valley, as Longs Peak and the nearby 13,000-foot peaks soar overhead.

At the signed intersection, take the turn to the southwest and traverse the eastern slope of 13,281-foot Mount Lady Washington on good trail, keeping your feet high as the terrain becomes slightly more rugged. The trail then descends slightly before regaining elevation to Chasm Lake, with the awe-inspiring summit of Longs Peak looming overhead to your south.

Weather permitting, doing this run at sunrise or sunset will yield especially magical views. On winter and spring days, this run may be accessible only to the Chasm Lake turnoff. The popularity of the area means there is often an established "trench" in snow, starting at the trailhead—thanks to snowshoers, backcountry skiers, and alpine climbers. However, if running this route in snowy conditions, it is highly recommended to bring microspikes for traction and to turn around at the Chasm Lake turnoff at 3.4 miles, making for a round-trip run of 6.8 miles total. This is because the final 0.7 mile of the route in winter crosses steep snow slopes where a slip and fall would be dangerous. If it has snowed more than a foot recently, the slopes above and below this section of trail also have avalanche potential.

The final approach to the lake crosses a flat section of the Chasm basin before ascending a few rocky switchbacks.

CHASM LAKE

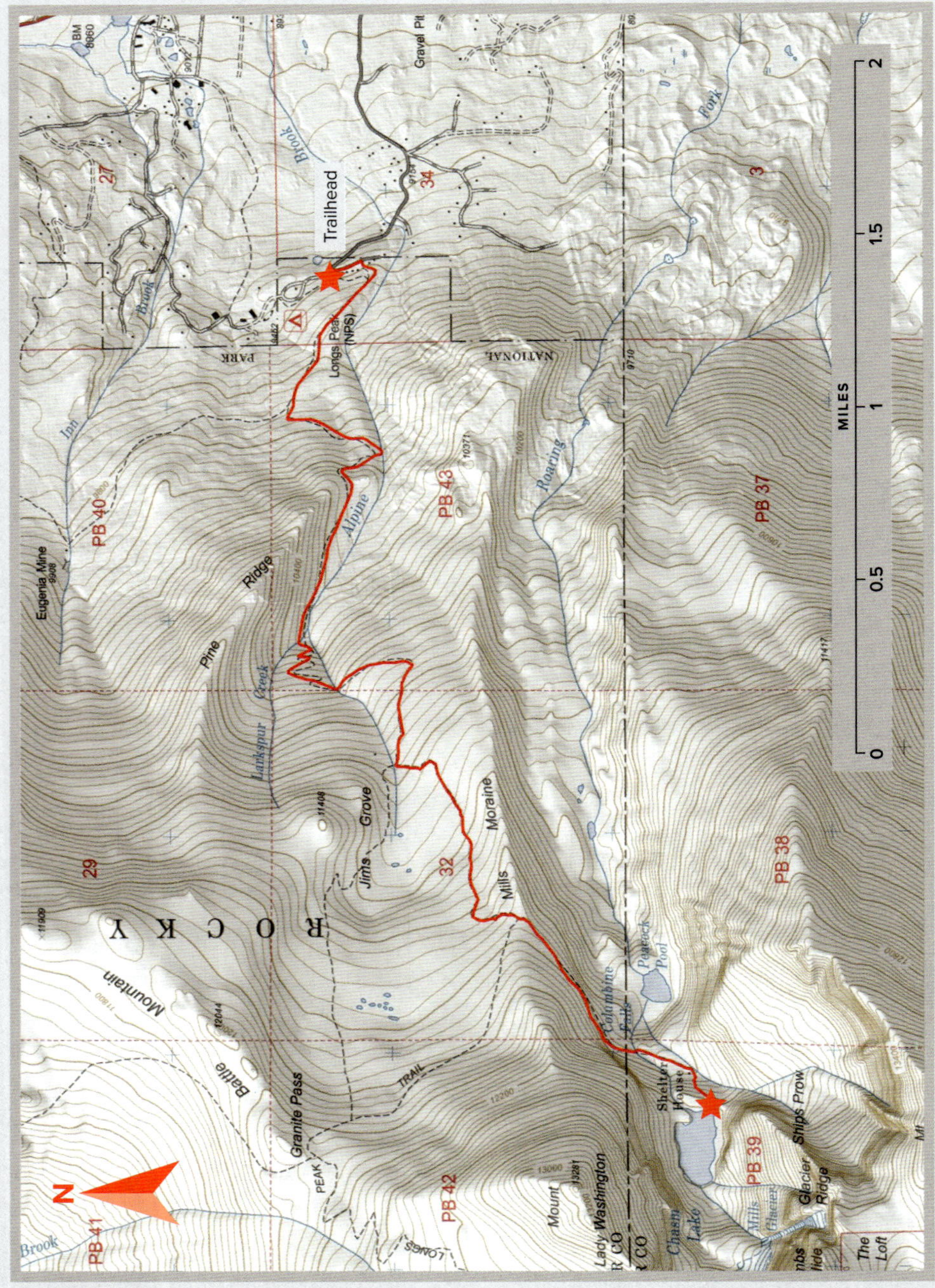

COLORADO ALPINE TRAIL RUNS

BLUE LAKE AND MITCHELL LAKE

2

Total Distance	7 miles (out-and-back)
Starting Elevation	10,350 feet
High Point Elevation	11,385 feet
Total Elevation Gain	1,190 feet
Difficulty	● Beginner
Round-trip Time	1.5–2 hours
Runability	100%
Nearest Town	Ward

COMMENT: This delightful lake jaunt is an east-west out-and-back route that starts in thick, coniferous forest and reaches tree line at Blue Lake, with a spectacular view of 12,979-foot Mount Toll. This run can be especially lovely in late spring or early summer when the trail has some snow and the lakes still hold some glacialesque ice. Because the run hovers in the low 11,000-foot range, Blue Lake is a good acclimation run in preparation for higher-elevation summit routes.

Mount Toll looms over Blue Lake.

GETTING THERE: From Ward, follow CO Highway 72 as it heads north. After less than 0.1 mile, turn left onto Brainard Lake Road. Follow it for 5 miles to the Pawnee parking lot at Brainard Lake. This trailhead is accessible by road bike or mountain bike from Ward or Nederland if you would like to up the mileage for an extra challenge. Note that the parking lots at Brainard Lake require timed-entry permits for access during the summer months through recreation.gov. Alternately, you can run or bike from the Brainard Gateway Trailhead (3.3 miles from Ward on Brainard Lake Road), where no permit is required.

THE ROUTE: From the Pawnee parking lot, cross to the road alongside Brainard Lake and head 0.1 mile west to the Mitchell Lake Trailhead. Keep a wary eye for the moose that enjoy browsing in the willows near Brainard Lake.

There are many trails radiating out from Brainard Lake, so pay close attention in the first 0.5 mile and maintain a west-northwest bearing from the first trail fork to the next intersection (0.2 mile). Continue straight for another 0.2 mile (instead of turning right or left) to the final fork, where the Mount Audubon Trail branches off to the right. Take the left-hand fork to continue up the valley for 3 more miles to reach Blue Lake.

After another 0.4 mile, you'll reach the first major creek crossing, which is an excellent photo opportunity with gorgeous wildflowers, rushing water, and boreal forest combining to give vivid illustration to the Eastern concept of "for-

Wildflowers alongside a creek crossing

If running this route in early summer, you may encounter a few snow br dges you must cross

est bathing." The broad creek crossing will test your balance as you rock-hop across before you resume a faster pace back on single-track. At Mitchell Lake, cross another, narrower creek as the forest thins and the trail wends its way farther west up the valley. Here, as trees become shrubs and willows and foot placements become slightly more technical, settle into a rhythm and enjoy the looming Indian Peaks around you.

These 2 miles pass by quickly, but upon reaching the slight basin that is home to Blue Lake, the stark backdrop of Mount Toll is sure to stop you in your tracks. Blue Lake is the largest body of water on this jaunt and a perfect spot for a snack break. Should you choose to run a little farther, Little Blue Lake is an additional 0 8 mile and adds another 450 feet of vertical gain.

Whether you choose to turn around at Blue Lake or Little Blue Lake, the descent on good, gradual trail flashes by. Make sure to pause occasionally to appreciate the beauty of your surroundings, or even take a mid-run dip into one of the lakes.

BLUE LAKE AND MITCHELL LAKE

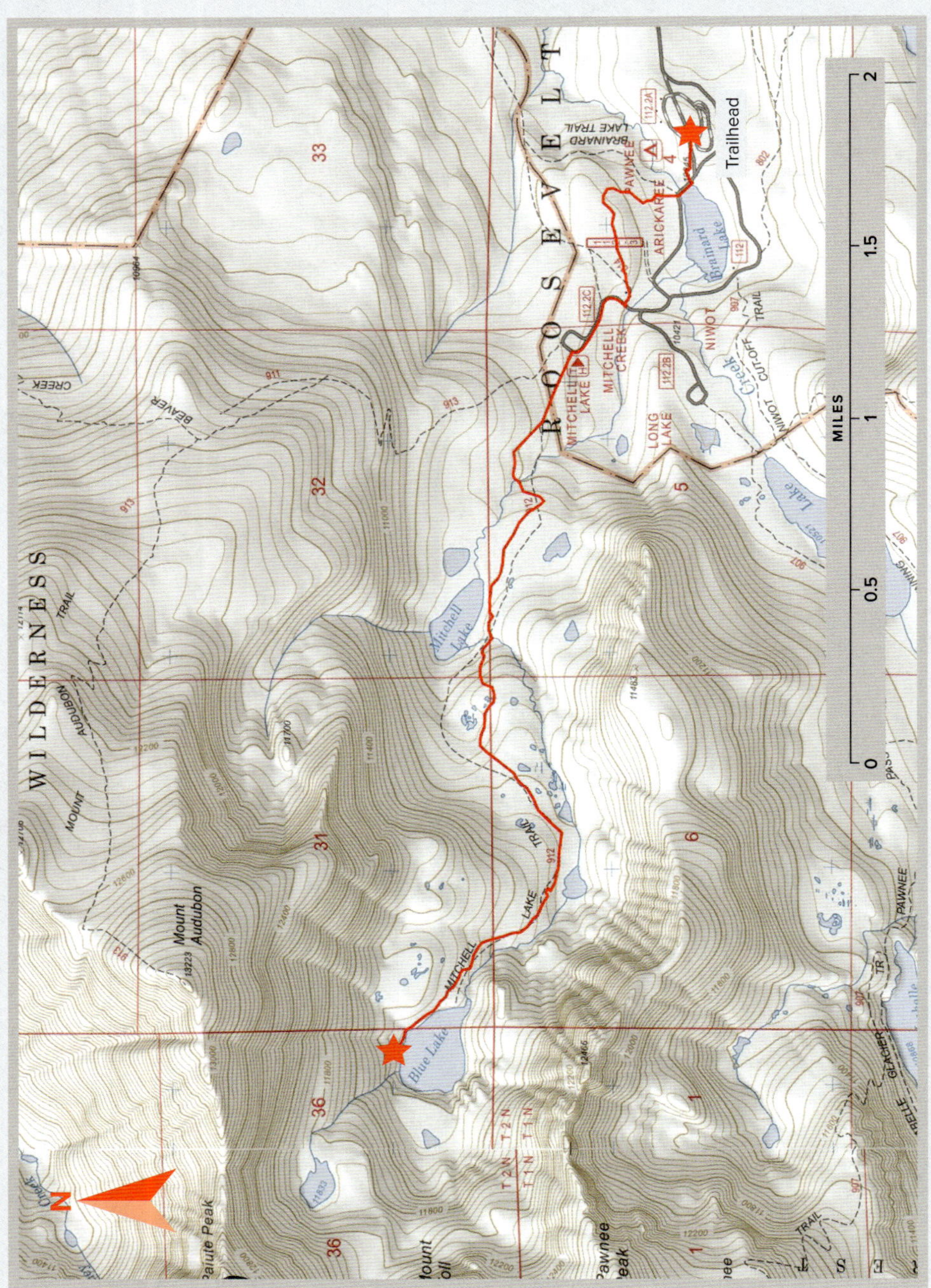

OLD BALDY

3

Total Distance	8.5 miles (out-and-back)
Starting Elevation	10,160 feet
High Point Elevation	13,039 feet
Total Elevation Gain	2,880 feet
Difficulty	■ Intermediate
Round-trip Time	1.5–2.5 hours
Runability	70%
Nearest Town	Nederland
Add-on	South Arapaho Peak (13,269 feet)

COMMENT: This summit route can be fit in before or after work by Front Range dwellers. It offers lovely views of both the gentle and dramatic features of the Indian Peaks Wilderness at the apex of the steady ascent. For early risers, it can be an excellent vantage point for sunrise over the eastern plains.

GETTING THERE: From Nederland, follow Eldora Road/CR 130 8.8 miles to the Fourth of July Trailhead. For the last 4 miles, 4WD is helpful. Trailhead access closes

The early section of the route heads up a broad glacial valley; morning and evening views are fabulous. Photo by Kate West

The view south from the summit offers a gentler perspective of the Colorado Rockies than some higher routes. Photo by Kate West

once the trailhead parking lots are full. This frequently happens by 6 a.m. on weekends, in which case you can park at Nederland High School and take the free shuttle to Hessie Trailhead and start the run there instead. This will add 7.6 miles and 1,060 feet to your round-trip.

THE ROUTE: If you have to start at the Hessie Trailhead, follow the dirt road upward and northwest for 4 miles until you reach the Fourth of July Trailhead. From there, head westward along the Arapaho Pass Trail for 2 miles. This section along the bottom of the valley can hold snow long into the summer; lingering snowfields are still referred to as the Arapaho Glacier.

At 11,230 feet, take a right at the trail fork to turn northeastward on the South Arapaho trail. Pace yourself mindfully on these switchbacks as you gain elevation. It is only 1.8 miles from the trail fork to the saddle between Old Baldy and South Arapaho peaks. Gain the saddle at 12,700 feet. Turn right (northeast) again, leaving the maintained trail. Only 0.3 mile and 340 feet remain to the broad, mellow summit. From here you have an excellent perspective of the dramatic traverse between South and North Arapaho Peaks to your northwest.

From the summit of Old Baldy, you can simply retrace your steps to return to the trailhead. However, should you want to add 0.8 mile and 230 feet to your round-trip route, you can bag a second summit with South Arapaho Peak. Once you return to the maintained trail, instead of descending, follow it westward. The terrain grows rockier and more technical, so choose footing carefully in this final stretch. Reach this second summit at 13,269 feet and 5.0 miles. In addition to the breathtaking and forbidding views of the Arapaho traverse to the north, you are now rewarded with the 4.3-mile descent back the way you came.

OLD BALDY

North Arapaho Peak
Indian Peaks Wilderness Area
South Arapaho Peak
Quarter to 5 Peak
Old Baldy
Arapaho Glacier Trail
Arapaho Pass Trail
0.7mi
0.4mi
0.3mi
1.8mi
0.9mi
0.2mi
0.5mi
0.6mi
1.1mi
4th of July
Roosevelt National Forest
Indian Peaks Wilderness Area
1.2mi
0.8mi
Trailhead
MILES
0
0.5
1
1.5

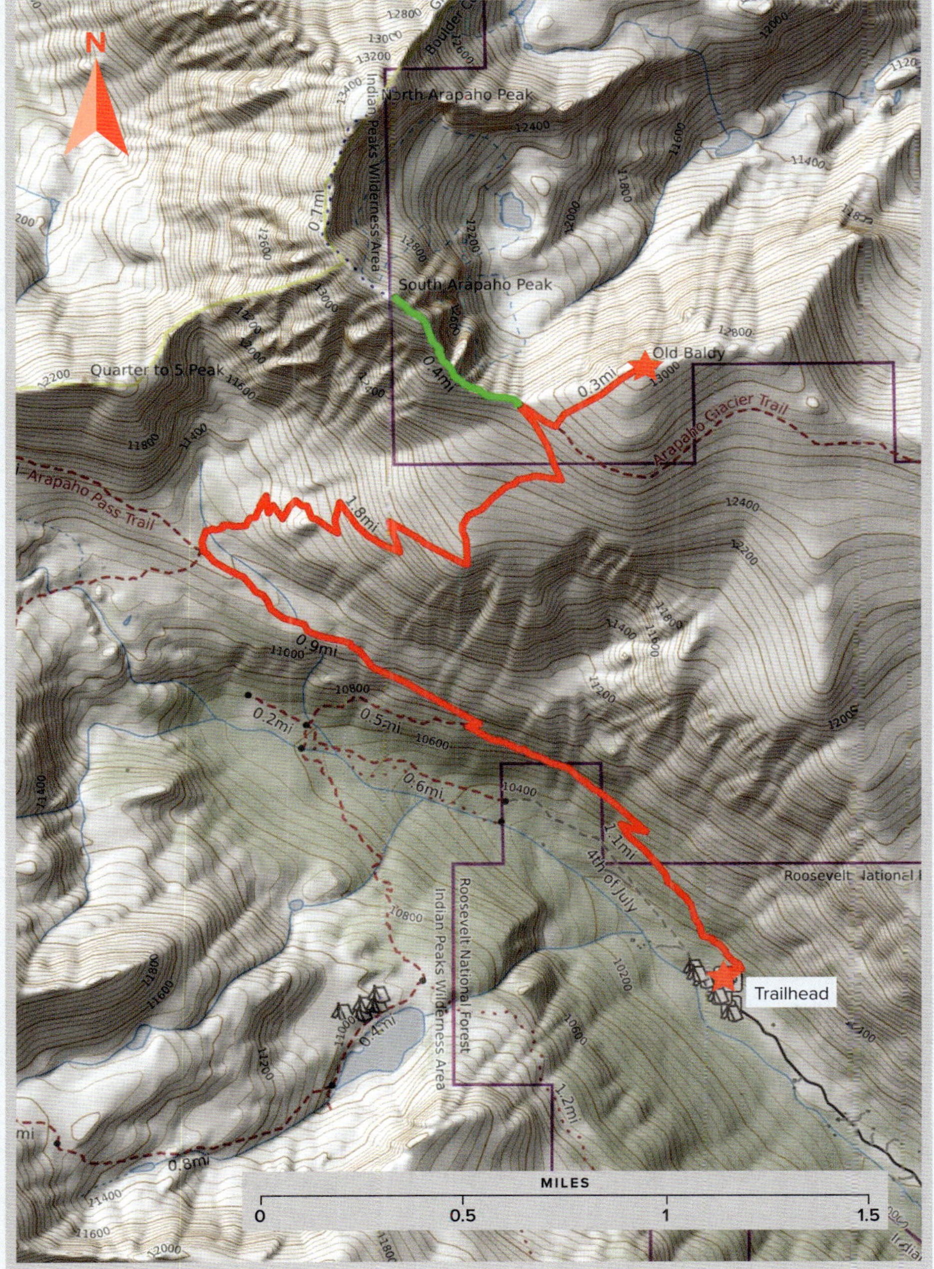

HIGH LONESOME LOOP

4

Total Distance	15.7 miles (loop)
Starting Elevation	9,000 feet
High Point Elevation	12,020 feet
Total Elevation Gain	3,560 feet
Difficulty	◆ Difficult
Round-trip Time	3–4 hours
Runability	80%
Nearest Town	Nederland

COMMENT: This loop takes you through two different, gorgeous valleys in the Indian Peaks Wilderness and along the crest of the Continental Divide. You'll pass several lakes and 12,000- and 13,000-foot peaks. This route is an excellent mid-distance run before progressing to longer routes or summit runs.

GETTING THERE: From Nederland, follow Eldora Road/CR 130 5.3 miles to the Hessie Trailhead. For the final mile, 4WD is helpful. On weekends, if you do not start early enough, direct access to the trailhead may not be possible and you may be required to park at Nederland High School and take the free shuttle to the Hessie Trailhead.

Reach the ridgeline at 6.8 miles and turn left (south) onto the High Lonesome Trail.

After passing King Lake (around mile 9), you may encounter some lovely wildflowers along the creek as you descend.

THE ROUTE: This route starts and ends along the broad, sandy Devils Thumb Trail. From the Hessie Trailhead, start at a steady jog heading due west. The first 1.3 miles are very gentle, gaining only 580 feet, mostly in a single ascent around the 1-mile mark. Reach your first trail juncture at 1.3 miles. Take a right onto Devils Thumb Bypass Trail rather than either of the other options, which involve crossing over the bridge and South Fork Middle Boulder Creek.

The next 1.5 miles paralleling Jasper Creek are also gentle, gaining just 420 feet to reach 10,000 feet at mile 3. Shortly before that, at mile 2.7, continue directly northwest on the Devils bypass trail rather than taking the sharp left. Along the section from mile 3 onward, contour steadily upward along the south-facing slopes of Chittenden Mountain (10,860 feet) and through the next tier of the Jasper Creek valley.

Reach Jasper Lake at mile 4.8 and 10,815 feet. The trail curves back to head due west as you get closer to the Continental Divide. Another 1.4 miles of gradual ascent remain

At 1.3 miles, take a right onto the Devils Thumb Bypass Trail and head northwest.

After turning left for the third time, pass King Lake and descend east back to the Hessie Trailhead.

to 11,270 feet, in which you'll pass the remnants of Devils Thumb Lake before your steepest ascent of the run.

From 6.2 miles, it is 0.6 mile and 710 feet to the saddle of the Continental Divide, just south of a nameless 12,116-foot point along the undulating ridge crest. Take a neat left turn south onto the intersecting High Lonesome Trail. You now have 2.4 southward miles that by trail running standards are flat, at or just below 12,000 feet.

At 8.8 miles, the trail begins curving southeast and losing elevation. At 9.3 miles, reach your next trail junction and take a left onto King Lake Trail. From here, head due north for 0.5 mile, dropping back to tree line as you pass along the picturesque east shore of the lake. At miles 9.8 and 10, stay right at trail forks to remain on King Lake Trail. You may want to pause at mile 10 to take photos as you cross South Fork Middle Boulder Creek. It descends enchantingly into the valley to the south here.

After this junction, keep high feet. The next 4.2 miles are a steady eastward descent to rejoin Devils Thumb Trail. Once you reach this junction, retracing your first 1.4 miles are all that remain back to the trailhead. Congratulations on what equates to a 25-kilometer and over 1,000-vertical-meter outing!

HIGH LONESOME LOOP

MOUNT SNIKTAU

5

Total Distance	3.8 miles (out-and-back)
Starting Elevation	11,990 feet
High Point Elevation	13,234 feet
Total Elevation Gain	1,800 feet
Difficulty	● Beginner
Round-trip Time	50 minutes–1.5 hours
Runability	80%
Nearest Towns	Silver Plume/Keystone
Add-on	Cupid Peak (13,117 feet)

COMMENT: This low, welcoming 13er is one of the few alpine routes that is accessible year-round, weather permitting. The summit offers a vantage of Torreys Peak in stunning immediacy to the southeast. A wind layer is a must. This route offers an excellent starting point for transitioning from trail running to high-altitude alpine running. While high in elevation, with the majority of the route between 12,000 and 13,000 feet, it is a well-trodden, easy trail and is one of the shortest routes in this guidebook.

GETTING THERE: Park at the summit of Loveland Pass, 4.8 miles up US Highway 6 West from Exit 216 off of I-70. Dogs are permitted on the trail on leash.

Trail crossing the broad Sniktau ridge

Northern couloirs of Torreys Peak from the Sniktau summit

THE ROUTE: Mount Sniktau starts steep from the small roadside parking lot. It gains 910 feet of its total vertical in the first mile. Since this is an extremely popular Front Range hike, the first mile of trail has been broadened and trampled by heavy foot traffic. To prevent further erosion, try to stay on the most heavily impacted section of trail. During snow season and from late spring to early summer, microspikes are valuable in navigating remaining snow.

Shortly before the 1-mile point, at about 0.9 mile, the trail turns left at a large cairn and heads northeast on single-track. The ridge here is rolling and wide, and the mile from the turn to the summit is deceptive; you'll pass over many false summits along the trail. When you reach a high point at which your GPS shows between 1.8 and 1.9 miles, you've finally arrived.

Sniktau can be quite windy given its proximity to the Continental Divide, so keeping a wind jacket easily accessible is recommended. In early summer, the route offers striking views of nearby ski areas (Arapahoe Basin to the south and Loveland to the west) as well as the twin 14,000-foot peaks of Grays and Torreys to the southeast. Some of these vistas include the jagged teeth of the Eagles Nest Wilderness to the west and a prominent 13er called The Citadel across I-70 to the northwest.

Cupid Peak, Mount Sniktau's neighbor to the south, can be added for 1.5 extra miles and 550 feet vertical gain round-trip on very similar terrain. Return to the large cairn at which you gained the ridge, then continue south along the trail for 0.75 mile to reach this second summit. The mellow and well-worn single-track between these two peaks makes for exhilarating, beautiful, and fast alpine running. After summiting Cupid, turn back northward and race back to the cairn, then descend back to Loveland Pass.

MOUNT SNIKTAU

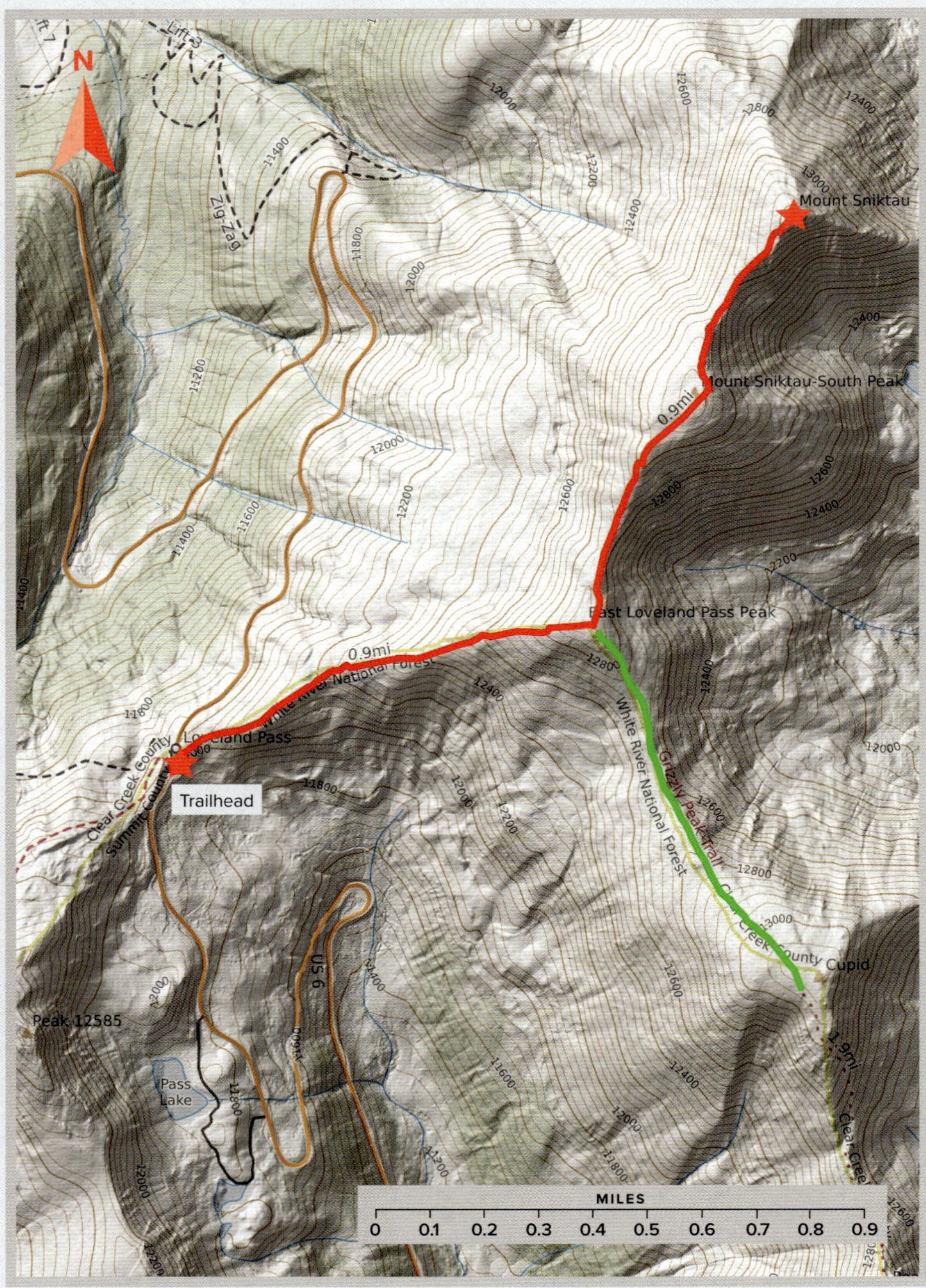

COLORADO ALPINE TRAIL RUNS

MOUNT FLORA

6

Total Distance	6.2 miles (out-and-back)
Starting Elevation	11,300 feet
High Point Elevation	13,140 feet
Total Elevation Gain	2,275 feet
Difficulty	■ Intermediate
Round-trip Time	1.5–2.5 hours
Runability	75%
Nearest Towns	Idaho Springs/Empire
Add-on	Colorado Mines Peak (12,392 feet)

COMMENT: A highlight of this run is the soaring views of the Gore Range to the west. Mount Flora's terrain makes for an excellent training run. It features a good single-track trail with rolling features that help wake up the legs, and plenty of broad boulders at the summit for runners inclined to sit or lounge while having a snack.

Looking north to Mount Flora from Colorado Mines Peak

Moody evening views along the trail

GETTING THERE: Take Exit 232 off I-70 and drive 15 miles northwest on US Highway 40 to the top of Berthoud Pass. Park in the large paved lot. This lot can also be reached by bike, though it is recommended that cyclists start their ride from Empire or Downieville. Note that although dogs are allowed, they must be on leash.

THE ROUTE: For just Mount Flora, start up the single-track that heads steeply up this old ski slope from the eastern edge of the parking lot. After 200–300 feet, the grade mellows and the path switchbacks through the forest. Once you leave tree line at 0.8 mile, you'll contour northward (left) along the slopes of Colorado Mines Peak to the saddle with Flora at 1.6 miles.

As the trail climbs farther, you'll encounter some switchbacks with loose gravel before the trail shifts to rolling single-track around 2.2 miles. This is largely a journey through colorful alpine meadows with dark rock outcroppings, delicate columbines in mid-summer and early fall, and stunning views of Rocky Mountain countryside.

The wide, flat summit remains out of sight until you are above 13,000 feet, at which point only 0.1 mile remains to the top. Remain patient, as the rolling trail can seem infinite. Though broad, the summit of Mount Flora is easily identifiable by

The author enjoying a summit sunset

the larger, tawny boulders strewn across it, which contrast with the smaller geology you've crossed to reach this spot.

During this gradual ascent, enjoy the moderately technical trail and the sharp western skyline. On particularly clear days, the horizon to the north frames gorgeous views of the wide Winter Park as well as ridgelines of Rocky Mountain National Park.

To include Colorado Mines Peak, start from the parking lot by jogging and power hiking up the dirt service road on the east side of the lot. This will lead you to the summit of the collegiate-titled 12er. This summit includes the scientific infrastructure of Colorado School of Mines in addition to providing a preview of the route to Mount Flora. This route adds 0.8 mile and 320 feet to your round-trip excursion.

MOUNT FLORA

Clear Creek
Grand County
Ethel Lake
Mount Flora
Mount Flora Creek
Grand County
Clear Creek County
Mud Creek
Peak 12,845
Mount Flora CDT
2.4 mi
Colorado Mines Peak
James Peak Wilderness Area
Arapaho National Forest
Mines Peak Trail
Grand County
Clear Creek County
Clear Creek Trail
Robert Creek
Fraser River
Arapaho National Forest Trail
US 40
US 40
US 40
Grand County
Clear Creek County
CDT tip
Trailhead
MILES
0   0.5   1   1.5   2
N

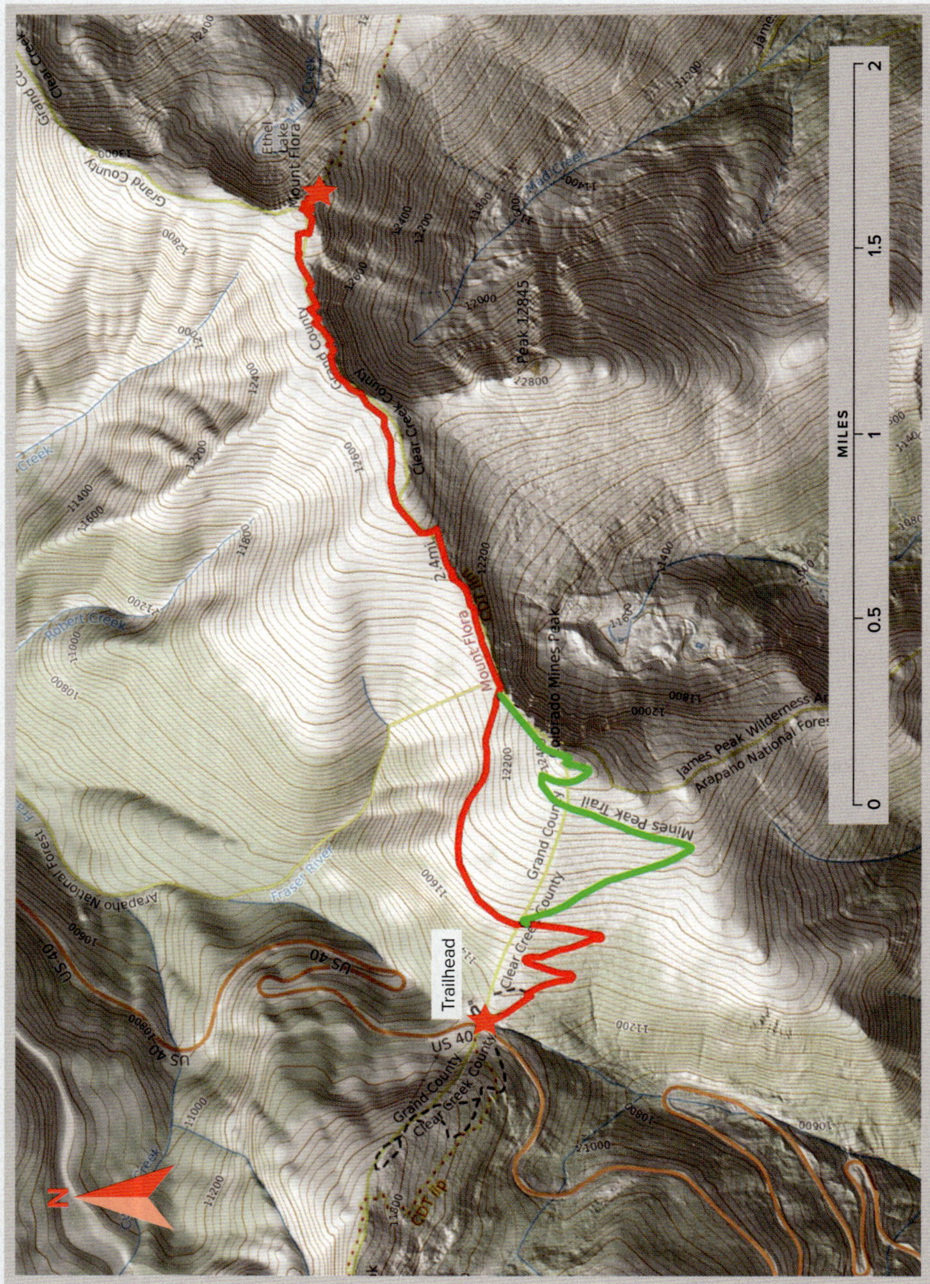

MOUNT BIERSTADT

7

Total Distance	7.5 miles (out-and-back)
Starting Elevation	11,500 feet
High Point Elevation	14,060 feet
Total Elevation Gain	2,775 feet
Difficulty	■ Intermediate
Round-trip Time	1.5–3 hours
Runability	80%
Nearest Town	Georgetown

COMMENT: Mount Bierstadt is one of Colorado's most popular 14ers. The gradual nature of the western slopes makes this trail an excellent training ground for high-altitude running, and it is quite popular for speed attempts. For those who live in the Front Range or Summit County in particular, the route makes for an excellent introduction to alpine running.

A runner ascends Bierstadt in early morning light.

Runners along the Bierstadt summit ridge

GETTING THERE: From Georgetown, drive 12 miles south on the beautiful Guanella Pass Scenic Byway. Watch for bighorn sheep, deer, cyclists, and the occasional moose while driving up this steep mountain road. Turn left at 12 miles into the official paved lot. This 2WD-accessible parking lot can also be reached by road bike, although be prepared for a long, steep haul. If the lot is full, park 0.1 mile farther up the pass in the Square Top lot on the right-hand side. Both the Bierstadt and Square Top lots have outhouses.

THE ROUTE: The first time I hiked Bierstadt, I studied the trail with wide, innocent eyes and started imagining what it would be like to run this amazing trail, fantasizing about taking bounding steps along winding alpine single-track.

Bierstadt's west slopes are a popular training ground for mountain runners, packing 2,600 vertical gain into just over 3.5 miles. It also usually hosts hundreds of hikers every summer day. In fact, one of the biggest obstacles to this run is starting early enough to avoid the crowds. On a weekday, starting between 4:30 and 5:30 a.m. should set you up for success. On a weekend, even earlier would be better.

Some runners may be interested in timing their start so that they summit at sunrise, and if so, they should know that the route from trailhead to summit takes between 1 hour and 1 hour, 45 minutes for most runners. On clear days, running

Alpenglow across the Guanella Pass 13ers

in the afternoon is one way to avoid the highest concentration of hikers. However, runners should *only* consider running this peak in the afternoon or evening with a good forecast and a strong skill at evaluating clouds.

Because the first mile loses 150–200 feet before starting the climb, running it is a nice, confidence-boosting warm-up. Once the climb begins at mile 1 (just after the shallow creek crossing), you may prefer to settle into a steady power hike, only occasionally breaking into a jog on flatter sections.

Take care to stay on the trail. Due to Bierstadt's popularity, the trail is wide and receives maintenance annually. There is ample room to pass other pedestrians without stepping off of the trail. This becomes especially important between miles 1.8 and 3, where the terrain is a combination of alpine tundra and rocky talus. Stepping off trail here contributes to rapid erosion, which is both highly damaging to the fragile ecosystem and makes for the highest-risk section of trail, with stretches of loose dirt, gravel-like pebbles, and rivulets of ice in the early morning.

From mile 3 to 3.5, the trail turns northeast (left), and large boulders along the summit ridge allow for a choose-your-own-adventure approach to the summit. Follow your preference as you scramble up these final 450 feet, perhaps pausing for alpenglow and sunrise photos if running in the early morning. From this narrow summit, relish the view across the Abyss valley to Mount Evans, the lovely green

A mountain goat grazes in the alpine tundra

alpine meadows on the peaks to your west, and the distant view to the Denver metropolis. The jagged Sawtooth ridge looms to your north, a spicy traverse for a non-running day, with helmet on head.

The Bierstadt descent takes 40–50 minutes for fleet-footed downhillers. Slower runners will average closer to 1 hour. Take particular care from the summit back down to 13,500 feet as you again navigate the large boulders. If you're a morning runner, the descent offers a wonderful opportunity to take in the early morning light across Guanella Pass and the glow on the east faces of nearby Grays and Torreys.

Be sure to give other trail users plenty of warning when passing. A clear and pleasant "Mind if I pass through?" gives hikers better notice of your gravity-boosted momentum. Remember to stay on the established trail. Keep feet high and light, particularly while descending the rocky sections from mile 4 to 5.7. Retain some reserves in your legs for the final, gradually uphill mile. The 530 final feet of gain in the homestretch feel like much more. Tag the trailhead sign before congratulating yourself in the parking lot. Or turn around and do it again, if you dare.

MOUNT BIERSTADT

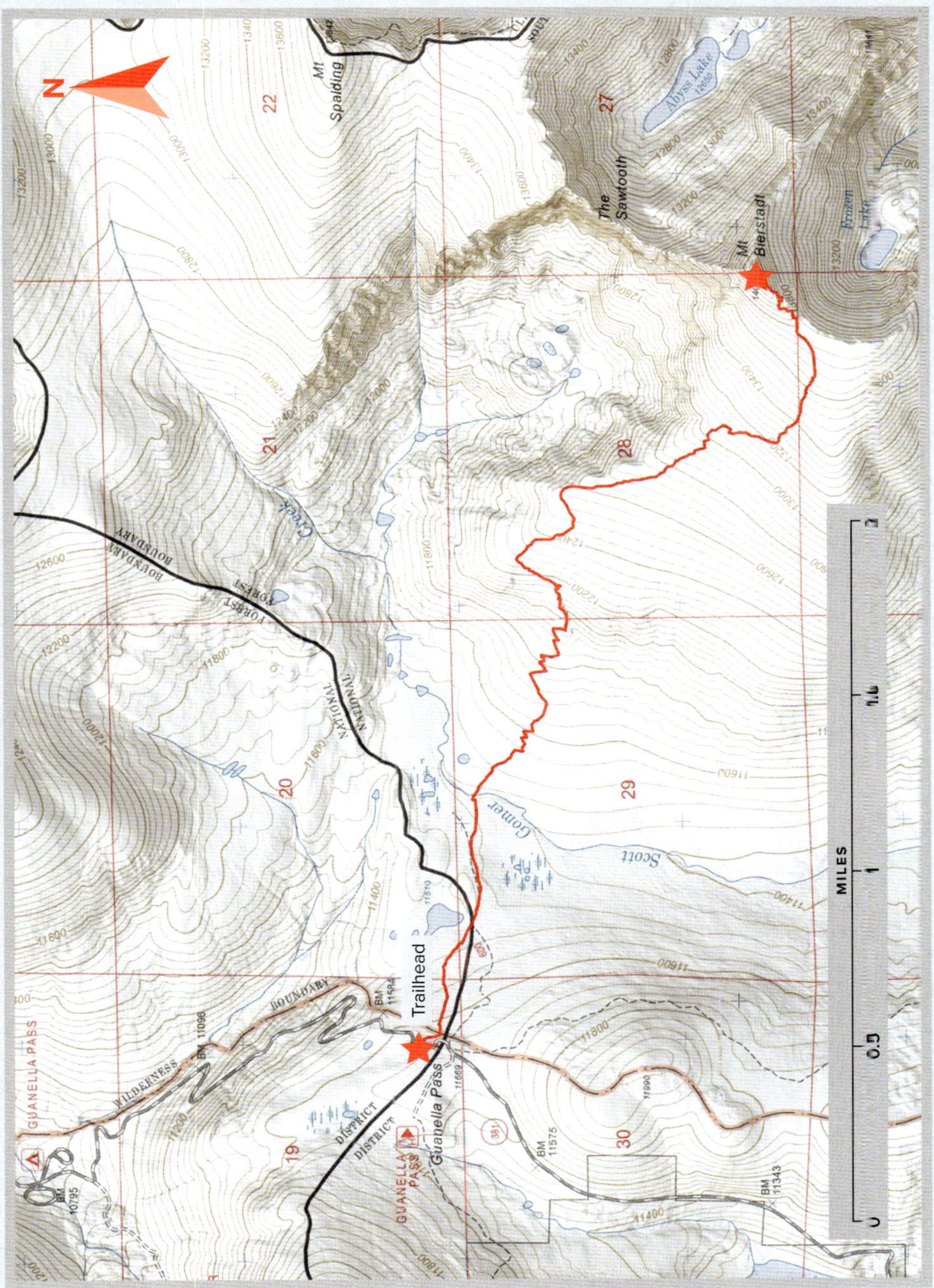

GRAYS AND TORREYS PEAKS

8

Total Distance	8.5 miles (out-and-back)
Starting Elevation	11,250 feet
High Point Elevation	14,270 feet
Total Elevation Gain	3,650 feet
Difficulty	■ Intermediate
Round-trip Time	2–4 hours
Runability	75%
Nearest Towns	Silver Plume/Dillon

COMMENT: Grays and Torreys are easily accessible from the Front Range and Summit County, so it's no coincidence that they are two of the most popular 14ers in Colorado. Running this route is an excellent way to make an easy hike more exciting. Route direction is up to you; the run in this book describes Grays to Torreys. However, either peak can be summited first before you head to the other. These peaks are runnable for much more of the year than most 14,000-foot peaks—from June to late November with good weather.

Wildflowers along the broad and level Stevens Gulch Trail early on your ascent

Left: In July and August, columbines decorate the side of the trail. **Right:** The traverse over to Torreys Peak from the summit of Grays at dusk

GETTING THERE: From I-70, take Exit 221 (Bakersville), 7 miles west of Georgetown and 16 miles east of Dillon. If your vehicle has at least 8 inches of clearance and 4WD, head south 3 miles on Forest Road 189 (Stevens Gulch Road) to the upper trailhead. Otherwise, park in the Bakersville exit dirt parking lot and add 6 miles and 1,450 vertical feet to your run.

THE ROUTE: The first 1 mile up the belly of the Stevens Gulch basin is on excellent, well-maintained trail. Don't let this fool you into thinking this section is flat, though; there's still 700 feet vertical gain to be had over this distance. In midsummer, Indian paintbrush and fireweed pop up here and there among the willows.

Passing by Kelso Mountain on your right, you begin to climb above the willows and the trail transitions to talus. At 1.9 miles and 12,300 feet, take care to continue heading westward on the main trail toward Torreys Peak rather than taking the right-hand fork, which leads to the technical Kelso Ridge, an exposed scramble that is not ideal for running. The main trail starts turning left (south) again shortly after this juncture to switchback up the north slopes of Grays Peak. It is 1.7 miles and 2,000 feet from the upper basin to the 14,270-foot summit up single-track talus.

After taking in views from the summit, enjoy a 0.5-mile reprieve northwest down to the Torreys saddle. From the 13,690-foot point, 0.4 mile and 580 feet remain to your second summit. From here, only downhill remains, so have a quick snack and drink before racing back down to the saddle. From the sign, take the short 0.3-mile connector trail back to the main trail. Your final 2.9 miles are on the same main trail on which you began, with gorgeous views of the Mount Edwards ridgeline to the southeast.

GRAYS AND TORREYS PEAKS

PIKES PEAK

9

Total Distance	25.1 miles (out-and-back)
Starting Elevation	6,690 feet
High Point Elevation	14,110 feet
Total Elevation Gain	7,545 feet
Difficulty	◆◆ Most Difficult
Round-trip Time	5.5–9 hours
Runability	70%
Nearest Town	Manitou Springs
Add-on	Top of the Crags Trail (0.4 mile)

COMMENT: This Colorado Springs classic is a long-standing running tradition in Colorado and for endurance runners worldwide. Home to the Pikes Peak Ascent and Marathon races, it is also a popular backpack for hikers interested in trying a Colorado 14er. While not an easy route, it is accessible and well-marked, and it offers the possibility of stopping at the summit house on top for a break and a variety of snacks and drinks. The route takes runners on a tour of the broad eastern slopes of the mountain, which is called Heey-otoyoo' and Tavakiev, respectively, by the Arapaho and Ute tribes that originally inhabited the area.

After 7.5 long miles of approach, arrive near tree line and move into more exposed, rocky terrain.

GETTING THERE: From I-25, take Exit 141 west onto US Highway 24 and follow it for 6 miles into Manitou Springs and all the way to the Barr Trailhead/Manitou Incline parking lot. If you arrive early enough, park here for a fee. If the lot is full, backtrack 1.5 miles to Memorial Park in downtown Manitou Springs and park in the lot on El Paso Boulevard, then take the shuttle to the Barr Trailhead. You can start your run from Memorial Park for an additional 2.8 miles and 370 feet round-trip.

THE ROUTE: The first several miles of the Barr Trail are very well-trod due to high traffic. The iconic Manitou Incline is nearby, and these early miles of the Barr Trail are the alternate descent route for the Incline hike. While the first 2.4 miles involve steady switchbacks, they are joggable and offer a good warm-up for the beginning of your day.

Pass the Manitou Incline connecter trail at 2.3 miles and 8,280 feet; continue westward. Shortly after this, the climate zone shifts as you move from sunbaked sage and pine to cooler, denser mixed forest with aspens and lush undergrowth. The trail navigates gently rolling terrain for the next several miles as you ascend the lower slopes of Pikes Peak. Pass through several clearings around 9,000 feet.

At 10,180 feet and 6.5 miles, reach Barr Camp. This charming log cabin has outhouses, a reliable stream with running water to refill bottles (treatment still necessary), and even a snack shop. This is an ideal location for a short break; once you leave Barr Camp, 1,100 feet remain to the upper reaches of tree line, at which point 4.6 sun-exposed miles remain to the summit.

One mile and 600 feet higher, spend some time on the northeast ridge before crossing southward again.

From the summit, take in the sweeping views to the north before starting the descent.

Once you exit tree line, take note of the unique terrain, with rosy, quartz-streaked boulders decorating this broad eastern face. The trail settles into long switchbacks of about 0.2 mile each, although one is a full 0.8 mile. On clear, breezy days, you might catch a glimpse of paragliders drifting in the sky above you. As you move steadily up these switchbacks, make sure to drink enough and consume adequate electrolytes; the high elevation and sun can easily drain you. Reapplication of sunscreen is also recommended.

As you approach the summit, you'll start to hear the hubbub of tourists from the Pikes Peak Cog Railway and the road. The large and looming Pikes Peak Summit House is a popular tourist destination and a welcome pit stop to celebrate the halfway point of your journey. Before heading inside, you may choose to continue west across the broad summit on the top of the Crags Trail (which approaches the peak from the northwest side of the mountain) for views down the dramatic gullies of the north face and across the Devils Playground for geological features on the northwest shoulder of the mountain. These views will add 0.8 mile to your round-trip distance.

After refreshing yourself with liquid and food at Pikes Peak Summit House, shake out your feet to start racing back down the Barr Trail. Be sure to engage your quads to support you on this 12.5-mile descent. Especially if it is a hot day, remember to take a few breaks when you are back below tree line. On your return to the Barr Trailhead, congratulate yourself: you just completed one of the hardest marathons in the United States!

PIKES PEAK

SUMMIT COUNTY

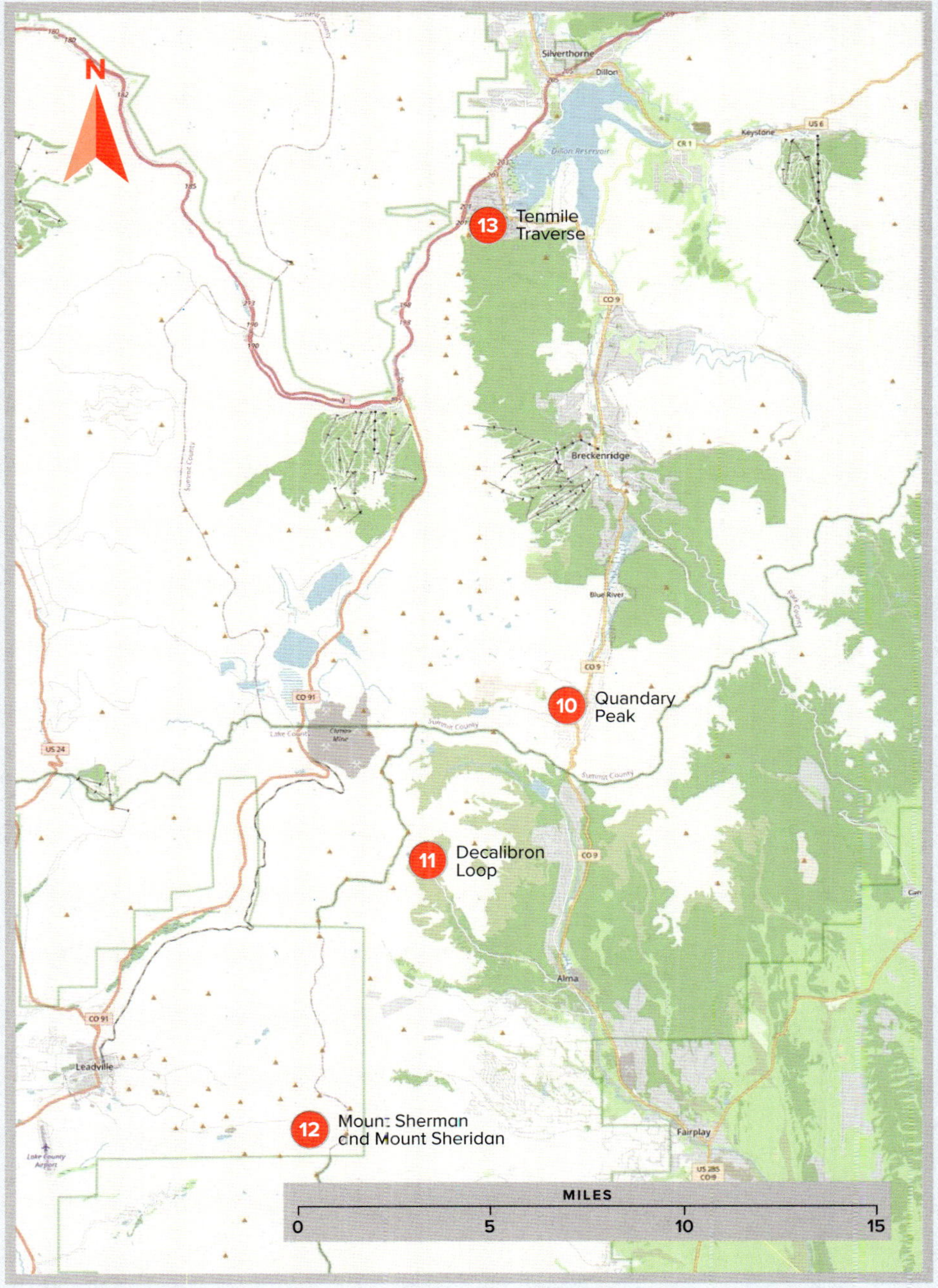

QUANDARY PEAK

10

Total Distance	7 miles (out-and-back)
Starting Elevation	10,850 feet
High Point Elevation	14,265 feet
Total Elevation Gain	3,450 feet
Difficulty	■ Intermediate
Round-trip Time	1.75–3 hours
Runability	60%
Nearest Town	Breckenridge

COMMENT: Quandary is consistently one of the most visited 14,000-foot peaks in Colorado, and it is technically runnable year-round for those who wish to try. Its east ridge is easy and popular. As with Bierstadt, a pre-dawn or late afternoon start will help you avoid foot traffic.

GETTING THERE: In summer and fall, the town of Breckenridge requires parking permits for the Quandary Peak Trailhead. Permits can be purchased in advance at parkquandary.com. A 3-hour permit is $5, but if you are not confident that you can complete the run in under 3 hours, you should consider paying for a $20 half-day

Early morning light on the summit as seen from below tree line

Some of the striking views near the summit of Quandary Peak include the Mayflower ridgeline connecting to Atlantic Peak to the northwest.

pass. Alternately, you can park at the Breckenridge Airport Lot and take the free shuttle to the McCullough Gulch Trailhead. The shuttle runs every 30 minutes from 5 a.m. to 6:30 p.m.

If you pay for a permit, drive 8 miles south from Breckenridge on CO Highway 9 to the parking lot at the base of Hoosier Pass. Turn right onto Blue Lakes Road and park in the large dirt parking lot just after you turn off of CO 9 rather than drive 0.25 mile to the small summer McCullough Gulch parking lot. The Quandary Peak Trailhead is accessible by bike from Breckenridge; a bike lock is recommended.

THE ROUTE: Though on the shorter side in terms of mileage, Quandary has fairly consistent vertical gain. Pace yourself accordingly. From the Blue Lakes parking lot, head north along McCullough Gulch Road (CR 851) for 0.3 mile. Turn left off of the road at the clearly signed Quandary Peak Trailhead and make your way eastward into the trees. The first 1.3 miles carry you through boreal forest on a wide sandy trail. This gives time to warm up to the slope grade with a little extra oxygen.

Around 11,800 feet, the conifers thin out and the trail transitions to rockier single-track through scree fields and patches of willows. It is common to see mountain goats in this area. If running with dogs, it is essential to have them on leash for their own safety in addition to regulations.

Around 12,150 feet and 1.6 miles in, the willows begin to disappear and the trail transitions to the alpine rockiness it maintains to the summit. Beware the plateau

The view west at the upper stretch of Quandary

around 13,000 feet (2.3 miles). You will not be able to see the actual summit until atop this bench, and seeing how much farther you have to go hits hard if you allow yourself to fantasize about the summit too early. Instead, enjoy the cardio effort and focus on the minutiae of the alpine flora as you pick your way up this east–west ridge.

At the end of this plateau (2.6 miles), the slope grade ticks up again noticeably. Most will want to power hike the last 1,000 feet up to the summit. The eye-catching Blue Lakes in the valley to the south provide a pleasant distraction as you propel yourself steadily upward. At the summit, pause to enjoy the views of the Tenmile Range rippling northward and the Mosquito Range meandering south. From this summit, several other classic alpine running routes are visible, including the iconic Tenmile Traverse (see p. 65).

Note that though Quandary has many routes, the East Ridge is the only non-technical route. Please do not attempt to run down any other routes. These routes are exposed, involve Class 3 to Class 5 climbing, or pose high risk for uncontrolled falls down snow and ice. If attempting this run in snowy conditions, microspikes are highly recommended. It is also recommended that you do not attempt to glissade Quandary in snow conditions without an ice ax.

QUANDARY PEAK

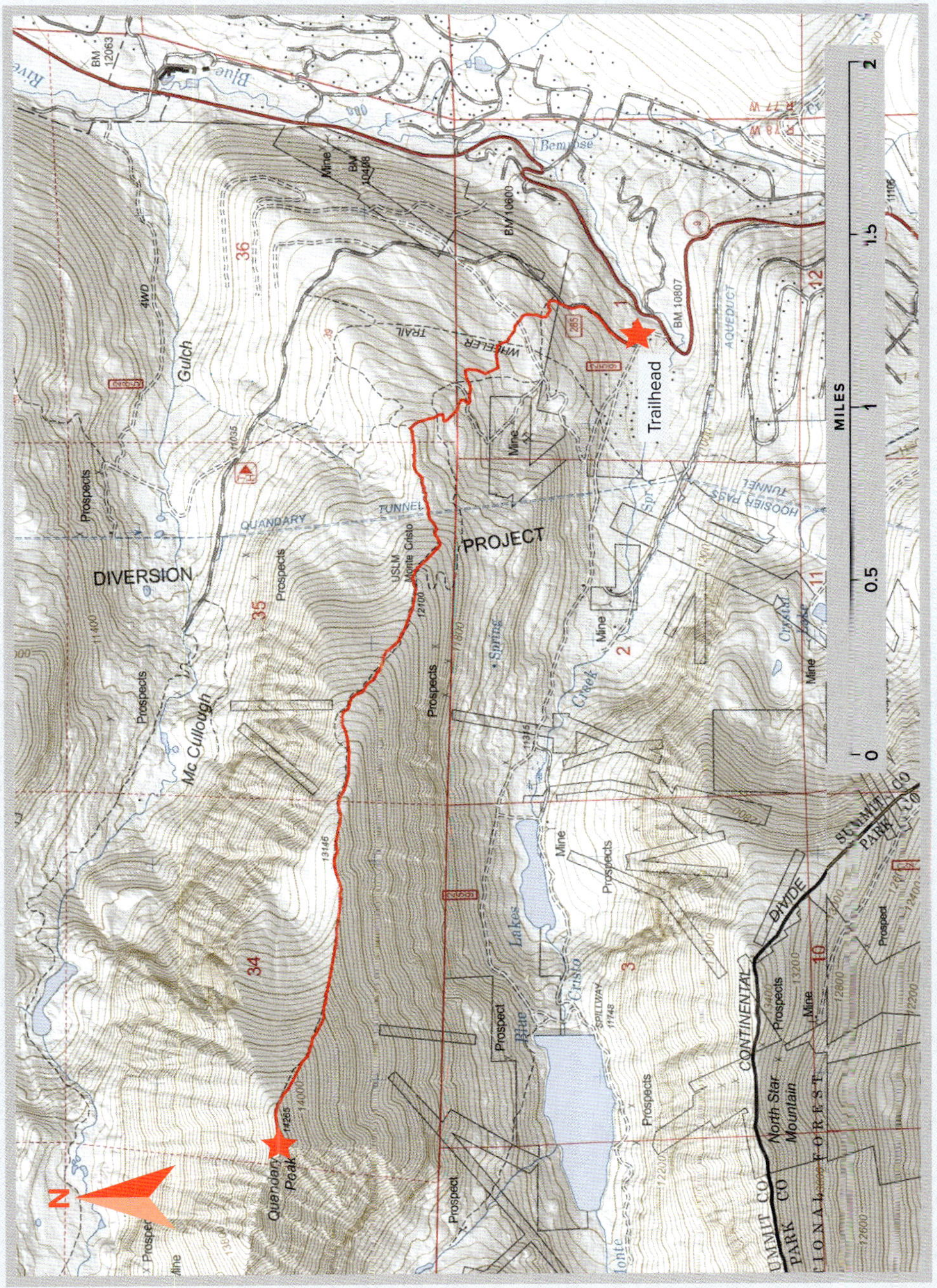

DECALIBRON LOOP

11

Total Distance	7.5 miles (loop)
Starting Elevation	12,000 feet
High Point Elevation	14,286 feet
Total Elevation Gain	3,400 feet
Difficulty	■ Intermediate
Round-trip Time	2–3.25 hours
Runability	70%
Nearest Town	Alma

Please note that the Decalibron area is a patchwork of public and private land. Access may be limited in some areas and users should respect all closures and private property boundaries. Stay on designated trails and confirm current regulations before visiting this area as access may change.

COMMENT: Decalibron is a popular loop connecting four Class 2 14,000-foot peaks. It can be done clockwise or counterclockwise from Kite Lake. This description recommends going counterclockwise so as to descend on the best-maintained trail.

The peaks of Mounts Democrat, Lincoln, Cameron, and Bross are private property and many segments of the Decalibron loop cross through mining claims. The owner of Mounts Democrat and Lincoln has generously granted access to the peaks, provided hikers stay on the designated trail, follow Leave No Trace principles, and avoid the summit of Mount Bross, which is closed to public access. Be sure to check with the Forest Service, South Park Ranger District, about the status of the trail and peak access. Please respect all closure and No Trespassing signs.

It is important to recognize that one of the summits, Mount Bross, is private property to which the public does not have legal access. The trail has clear signs for the bypass at mile 1.5 (at around 13,940 feet) over to Mount Cameron and Mount Lincoln. The author and the Colorado Mountain Club are not liable should you choose to not follow these signs.

Northern views from the summit of Mount Democrat

GETTING THERE: From Alma, turn west (left if you are driving north) off of the main street at the Kite Lake sign. Follow the dirt road (CR 8) for 6 miles to the Kite Lake Trailhead. As this is an extremely popular group of mountains, it may be necessary to park up to 1 mile down the road. Kite Lake Trailhead is 2WD-accessible with at least 8 inches of clearance. It can also be reached by mountain bike, but the only potential places for locking bikes are the picnic tables next to campsites. This trailhead is privately owned and maintained by a partnership with the US Forest Service and Town of Alma. A $2 to $10 fee is charged through self-issued parking permits. The Kite Lake Road is closed to vehicles in winter and spring to minimize road damage. Contact the US Forest Service South Park Ranger District for current road information.

THE ROUTE: To start, head toward the Mount Bross bypass trail and take the right-hand fork shortly beyond the Kite Lake trail sign. Follow this trail east and then northeast as it winds from the alpine meadow around the lake up the loose, talusy rib of Bross. Around 12,200 feet (0.3 mile), the grade becomes consistently steep. You may prefer to power hike this section. Eventually, the switchbacks bring you to the ridge-edge of this rib, and at around 13,800 feet the trail becomes more gradual and joggable again as it heads north.

The trail stays high for 2.5 miles as it traverses side slopes and goes out and back along the Mount Lincoln ridge. This section is particularly breathtaking, with cliffs dropping away to the east and steep slopes rolling away to the northwest. The yellowy-red rock passes through old mining sites and claims, offering a fun glimpse into Colorado history.

At the 2.6-mile mark, your traverse reaches the narrow Lincoln summit ridge that makes a particularly breathtaking spot for alpine running photos. Be mindful of hikers, as this area of great exposure can bring up nerves for those with acrophobia. Lincoln's summit, at the 3-mile mark, offers excellent views of the Tenmile Range Centennial peaks and 14er Quandary Peak.

Heading south again to Mount Cameron is 0.5 mile on easy and gentle terrain. The narrow Lincoln ridge broadens to a large, flat expanse; only the summit cairn helps to discern this unofficial 14,000-foot summit.

After conquering Mount Cameron, the route gets more technical and exciting. Keep your feet high and light as you navigate steep switchbacks 800 feet and 0.9 mile down to the saddle with Mount Democrat. This stretch of trail is exhilarating, and quick reflexes are a huge asset here as you bound over the larger rocks in the winding single-track. Tap into flow state to fly down the trail with lightning focus.

Mount Cameron and Mount Lincoln as viewed from the bypass trail on the shoulder of Mount Bross

A runner approaches the trailhead after completing the route.

At the saddle, switch gears to power hike up the final peak. This 740-foot climb over the space of 0.6 mile will have your legs burning. Be cautious on this initial steep section of your final descent, then stretch out the legs for the easier last 2 miles back to the trailhead. The final 0.5 mile through gradual alpine meadow alongside Kite Lake will feel triumphant; relish this and celebrate your run and the striking backdrop!

DECALIBRON LOOP

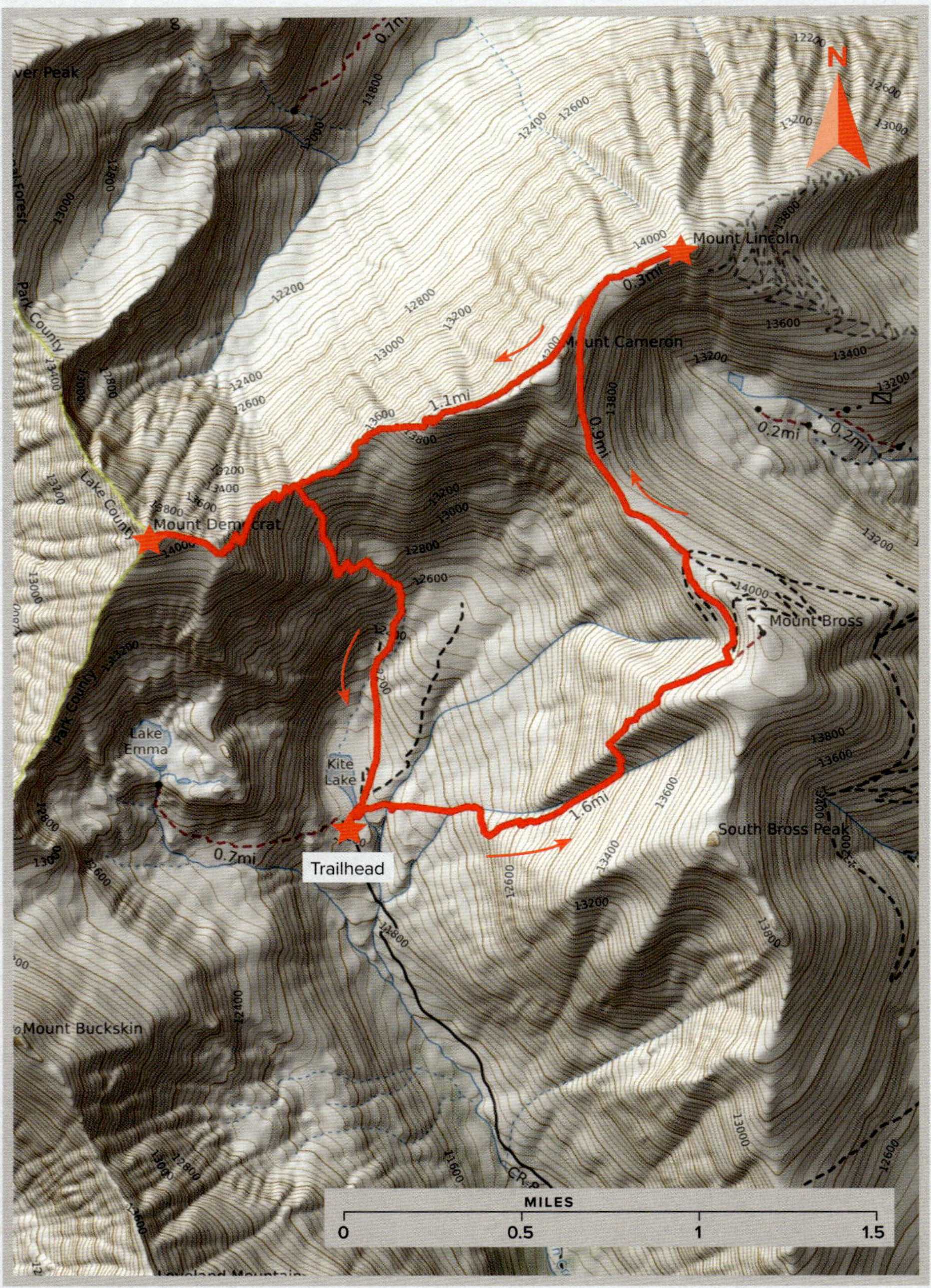

MOUNT SHERMAN AND MOUNT SHERIDAN

12

Total Distance	6.5 miles (out-and-back)
Starting Elevation	12,000 feet
High Point Elevation	14,036 feet
Total Elevation Gain	2,750 feet
Difficulty	■ Intermediate
Round-trip Time	1.75–2.5 hours
Runability	60%
Nearest Town	Leadville
Add-on	Peerless Mountain (13,348 feet)

COMMENT: Mount Sherman is a well-known hike from the eastern Fairplay side, but its western side also looms over sections of the iconic Leadville Trail Marathon and Silver Rush ultra courses. This route offers a fun, challenging vertical-to-mileage ratio for those on a time budget.

Looking north at Mount Sherman and the Iowa Gulch 13ers from the summit of Mount Sheridan

GETTING THERE: From Leadville, drive south on Harrison Avenue and take a left onto Monroe Street. Your total driving distance from this initial turn will be 7 miles. After 500 feet, turn right onto County Road 2. Follow CR 2 for 3.8 miles to the County Road 2B turnoff on your left, where the road turns to dirt.

Continue following the road east for about 3.1 miles to the small parking lot on the right (south) side of the road. This is the Iowa Gulch Trailhead. At 12,080 feet, it is 2WD-accessible with at least 8 inches of clearance. If the lot is full, there is room to park on the shoulder of the road near dispersed camping spaces around the 5-mile mark (1–1.2 miles from where CR 2B turns to dirt). This will add 2 miles and 640 feet to your ascent. If you wish to mountain bike to this trailhead, you can park your car near the Circle K gas station in Leadville, 300 feet north of the first Monroe Street turn, and start your ride from there.

THE ROUTE: In late summer and early fall, Iowa Gulch is an oasis of high-elevation forest and alpine tundra. Start from the roadside parking lot at 12,080 feet and turn southeast onto the thin single-track. This footpath has a small sign and descends through willows toward the base of the valley. It can get muddy here. Cross Iowa Creek and start to switchback up into talus trail toward the 13,100-foot saddle between Sheridan and Sherman.

From the saddle (1.3 miles), turn south (right) and contour along the eastern side of Sheridan. As you near the saddle with Peerless Mountain, you'll find thin tread that switchbacks westward up toward the Sheridan summit, approximately 0.6 mile from the saddle. For those who want to extend their run, adding on Peerless is 1.1 extra miles and 200 extra vertical feet. This add-on is along picturesque alpine ridgeline that offers a gentle interlude to the more rugged terrain of the higher peaks. The faint trail here is very runnable and a good opportunity to frolic across the alpine tundra while getting a glimpse of some of the lesser-viewed basins in this part of the Mosquito Range.

If you do not choose to add the jaunt to Peerless, turn west and take the steep switchbacks up Mount Sheridan. This ascent gains 550 feet in 0.6 mile, so the going may be slow. Be mindful to keep high, light feet on your descent, as this trail is not as frequented as the Sherman ridgeline you will be ascending next.

Though this route is heavy on talus, it is a reasonably mellow mix of jogging and power-hiking terrain with sweeping views of South Park to the east and the Sawatch Range stretching along the western horizon. Although Sherman is notoriously windy, the southwest slopes are less so.

After traversing back to the saddle from Sheridan, power hike the final mile up the ridge to Sherman's broad summit. From this high point, it's a 2.5-mile, light-footed trip back down to the trailhead. If tackling this route early in the summer, you may have the opportunity to glissade stretches of snow next to the switchbacks from the saddle down toward Iowa Gulch.

Southwestern views from atop Mount Sherman

MOUNT SHERMAN AND MOUNT SHERIDAN

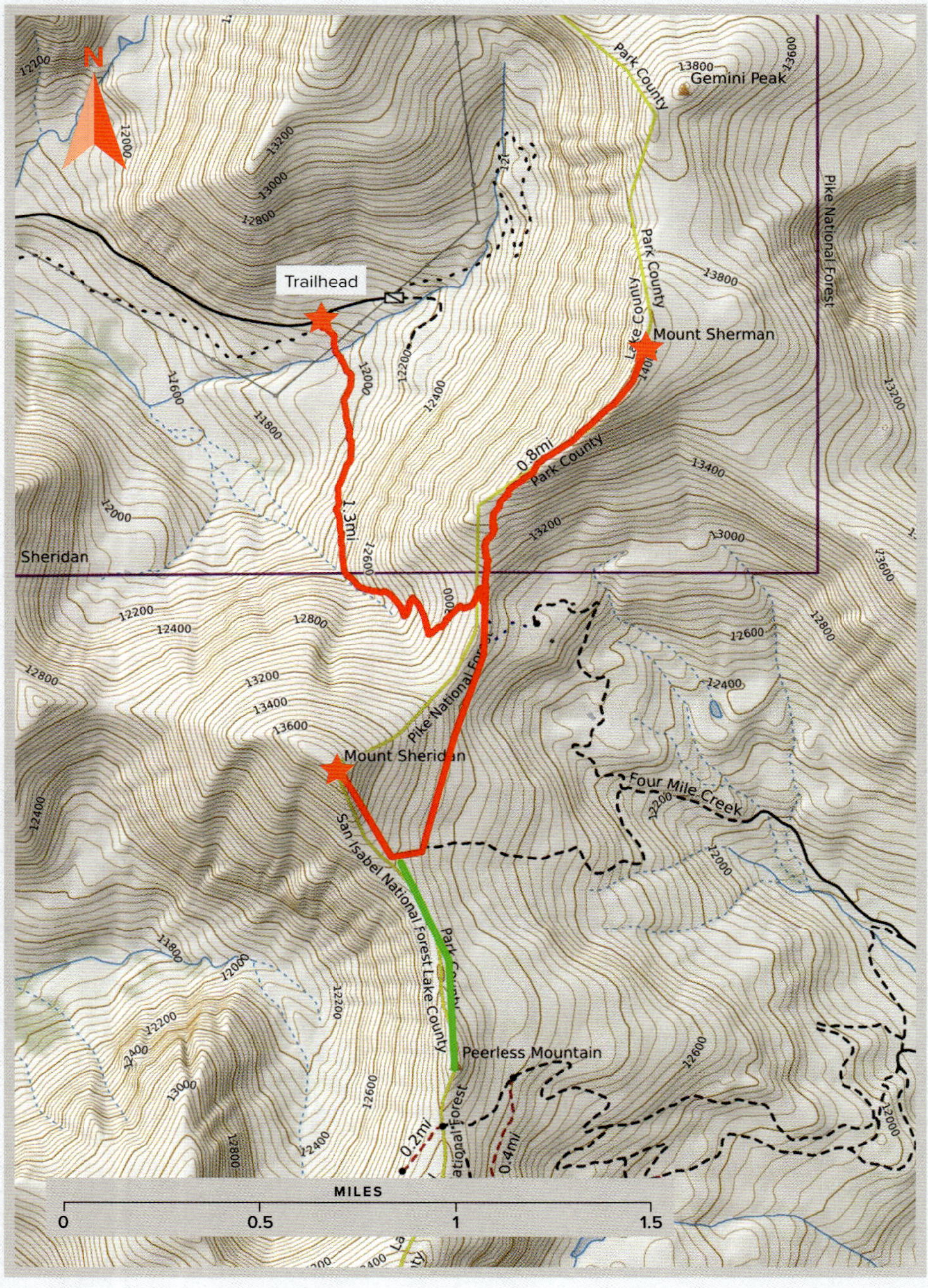

TENMILE TRAVERSE

13

Total Distance	14.7 miles (point-to-point)
Starting Elevation	9,165 feet
High Point Elevation	13,633 feet
Total Elevation Gain	8,320 feet
Difficulty	◆◆ Most Difficult (Note: Do not attempt this unless you are highly experienced with off-trail navigation and comfortable in mountaineering terrain.)
Round-trip Time	4.5–8 hours
Runability	70%
Nearest Towns	Frisco/Breckenridge
Add-on	Mount Royal (10,502 feet)

COMMENT: This Summit County classic takes you on foot from Frisco to Breckenridge, mostly along the crest of the Tenmile Range. It is technical, and significant sections are on social rather than maintained trails. A climbing helmet is recommended for the stretch from Peak 1 to Peak 4. The spectacular views and dozens of summits are best saved for once you feel quite confident in your alpine running and navigating skills. This route is best done in early autumn after monsoon season.

Left: On the narrow, rugged Class 3 terrain, be sure to wear a helmet and move forward carefully. **Right:** A closer look at the technical terrain on the ascent of Peak 4

Note: For more photos from the trailhead to Tenmile Peak and Peak 4 to Peak 10, check out the excellent trip report at 14ers.com/php14ers/tripreport.php?trip=15556.

Left: At the dragon's head, dip lower below the ridge crest on the west side for easier terrain.
Right: You can find Class 2 terrain here as you navigate past the dragon.

GETTING THERE: It is highly recommended to do this route as a point-to-point run with a car shuttle, and to start before sunrise. It's essential to have 4WD vehicles with 8+ inches of clearance. Drop a car at the Beaver Run SuperChair below Peaks 9 and 10 in the Breckenridge Ski Resort. This is 3 miles up the service road from the bottom of the lift and the town of Breckenridge. Take the second vehicle back down to Lower Sawmill, then head 12.2 miles to the small Rainbow Lake Trailhead in Frisco, off of South 2nd Street. Mount Royal Trail starts here. Check that you have plenty of water and food for the excursion. As most of this route is atop a ridgeline, there are no points at which to refill water.

THE ROUTE: Start up Mount Royal Trail, heading southwest and immediately gaining vertical. Mount Royal Trail steadily switchbacks up to the ridgeline, 1,250 feet of ascent in 1.3 miles. If you want to do the optional add-on of Mount Royal itself, turn right (north) for 0.3 mile (a 0.6-mile total addition back to the trail fork). If not, turn left (south) to head toward Mount Victoria and Peak 1; you'll soon leave tree line behind and won't see it again for the remainder of the traverse.

Gain the summit of Mount Victoria shortly after tree line at 2.4 miles and 11,785 feet. Continue on at a steady pace to reach Peak 1 at 3.2 miles and 12,805 feet; though the route remains clear, expect the trail after Mount Victoria to fade from maintained to social use. At the top of Peak 1, put on your helmet. From Peak 1 to Peak 2, also known as Tenmile Peak, the route is clear but more technical, with only a very faint social trail. Stay atop the ridgeline, descending 220 feet and then reascending 340 feet over 0.5 mile to reach the summit at 12,933 feet.

If you are not comfortable with exposed, off-trail terrain that requires scram-

Left: Look back at the dragon before tackling the remaining technical terrain to Peak 4.
Right: A runner navigates the knife-edge close to the top of Peak 4.

bling, turn around here and return the way you came for a total of 7.5 miles round-trip. The next 1 mile is the most technical and difficult of the day as you summit Peak 3 and then Peak 4. The difficulty can be kept to Class 3 scrambling, but this section is not runnable and you should be cautious as you routefind. Start descending from Peak 2 along the ridge crest, but as the ridge grows narrower and more technical, stick to the easier terrain just on the western, right-hand side. You should only occasionally need your hands for stability. The trickiest spot comes just after 4.1 miles at 12,600 feet, at a gendarme known as the head of the dragon. Here, you'll want to drop a little farther below the ridge crest on the west side, following the social trail on grassy ledges below the Class 5 scrambling (which is known as riding the dragon's back). This traverse should take only 0.1 mile before you regain the ridge, and you'll reach the summit of Peak 3 at 12,635 feet after another 0.1 mile.

From here, descend 0.2 mile and 235 feet on easier terrain on the top of the ridge. Only 0.3 mile and 440 feet of technical terrain remain, up the Class 3 knife-edge of Peak 4. Enjoy this exhilarating, airy section before stepping onto easier terrain at the 12,866 summit of Peak 4. You've gone 4.8 miles, just shy of a third of your total distance. Here you can remove your helmet; the majority of the rest of the route, including Peaks 5 through 8, is relatively gentle, runnable terrain heading due south along the ridgeline. The last real navigation comes after reaching Peak 9 at 10.1 miles (5.3 miles later). Instead of continuing due south down the ridge, turn southeast for 0.4 mile to catch the Fourth of July road. Once on the road, follow it 1.1 miles to your final summit of the route, Peak 10 at 13,633 feet. You're now at 11.6 miles; only 3.1 miles remain on obvious road. Enjoy the 2,200-foot descent back to your car at the Beaver Run SuperChair.

TENMILE TRAVERSE

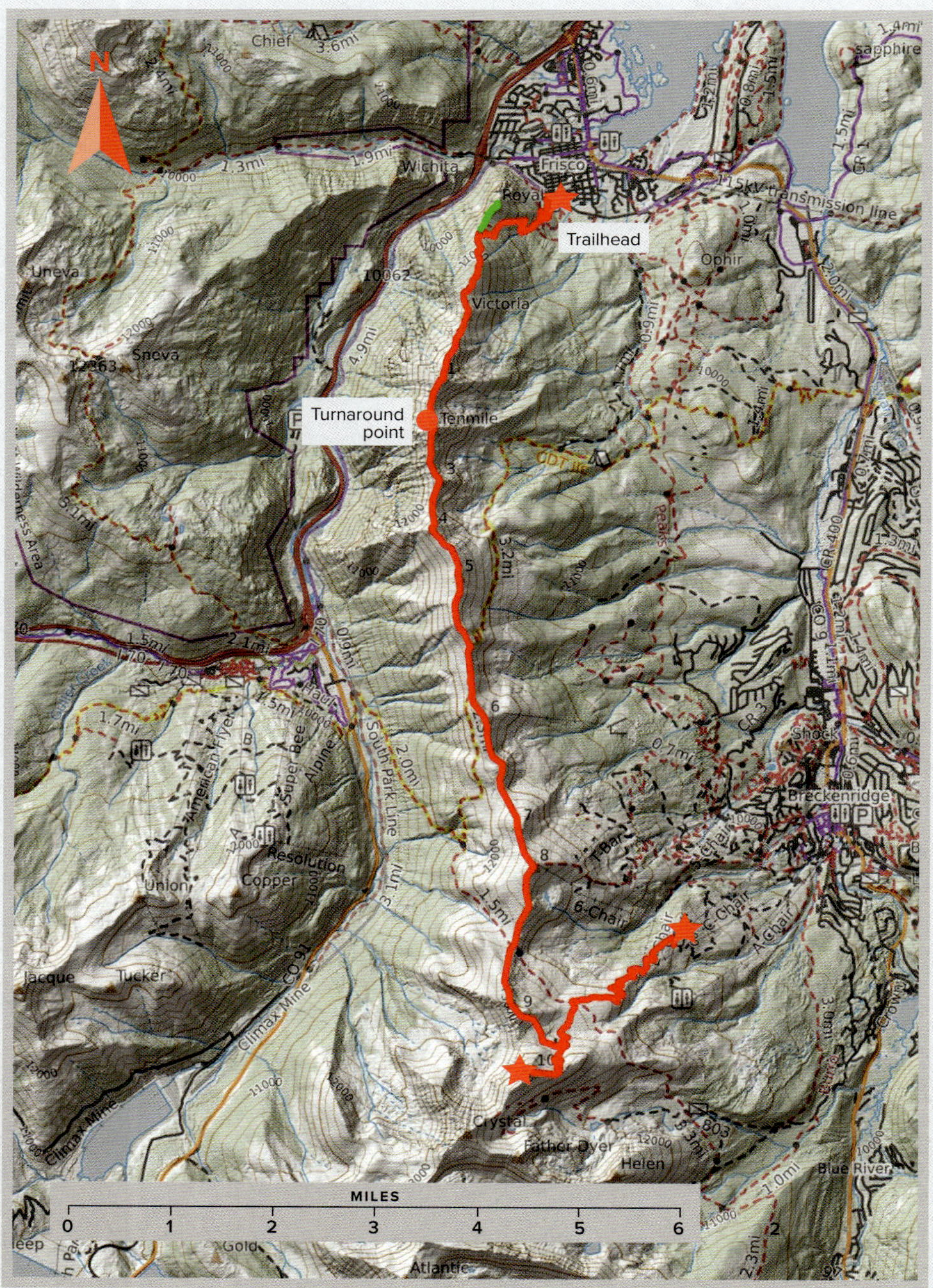

ELK RANGE

Mount Massive Wilderness Area
Lost Man Loop
15
Hunter-Fryingpan Wilderness Area
Midway Tarn
14
Electric Pass Peak and Leahy Peak
18
19
Aspen
Aspen Highlands
16
Aspen-Pitkin County Sardy Field Airport
Castle Peak
22
Four Pass Loop
21
Snowmass Three Pass Loop
17
Capitol Lake
20
Mount Sopris
Raggeds Wilderness
CO 82
CO 133
MILES
N

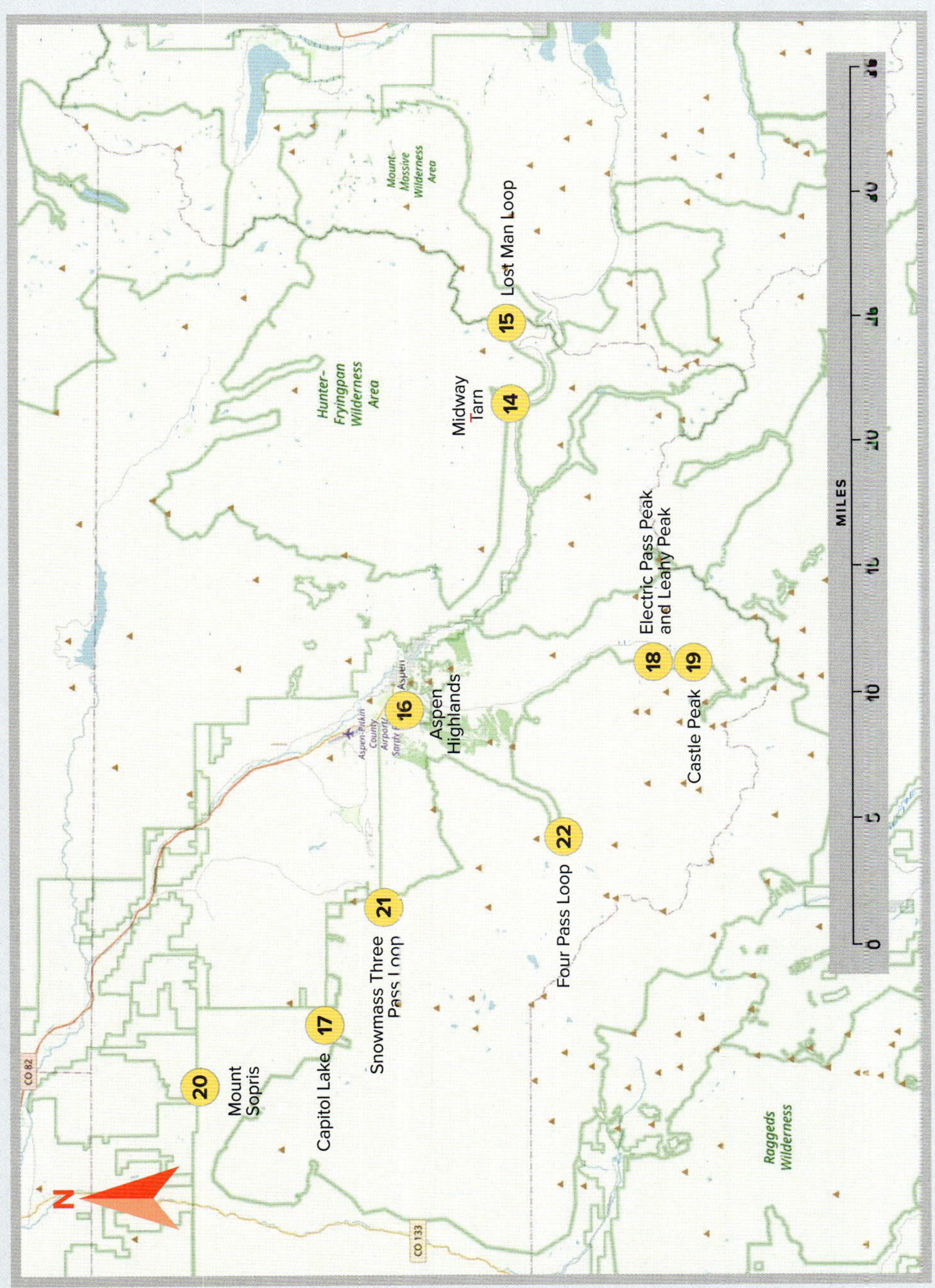

MIDWAY TARN

14

Total Distance	4.5 miles (out-and-back)
Starting Elevation	10,512 feet
High Point Elevation	11,995 feet
Total Elevation Gain	1,502 feet
Difficulty	● Beginner
Round-trip Time	45 minutes–1.5 hours
Runability	90%
Nearest Town	Aspen
Add-on	Midway Pass (Note: This route takes the difficulty to Black Diamond.)

COMMENT: When it comes to short, steep runs with spectacular views, Midway Tarn is unrivaled. Less trafficked than the Lost Man Loop, with which it shares a trailhead (p. 75), it features excellent single-track and a panoramic view of the Elk Mountains. It is popular among Roaring Fork Valley locals. This route is a great acclimation run before tackling the higher-elevation and longer routes in the Elk Range.

The upper switchbacks of the Midway Trail around dusk

Midway Tarn with the Elk Range stretching across the western horizon

GETTING THERE: From Aspen, drive 13.4 miles east on CO Highway 82 to the Lower Lost Man Trailhead. The trailhead parking is on the north side of the highway, while the south side hosts the Lost Man Campground. This is 23.1 miles from Twin Lakes and is 2WD-accessible. While this trailhead is accessible by bicycle, Independence Pass is extremely popular in summer months; cyclists should be prepared for narrow roads with cars passing frequently. Note that dogs are allowed but must be leashed.

THE ROUTE: Tarns are a geologic feature that linger in the aftermath of glacial recession, small ponds carved into flat steps by ancient ice. This particular tarn sits right at the upper limits of tree line in a stretch of alpine meadow that looks south and west across the Elks—the open, U-shaped valleys and jagged, crumbling peaks stretching away toward the desert. This is the ancestral territory of the Ute people.

The run itself is short and steep. After heading north 0.2 mile on the Lost Man Trail, take a left at the signed trail fork onto the Midway Trail. Start up switchbacks of broad, well-maintained single-track that carry you westward up out of the Lower Lost Man valley through well-spaced pine trees. Around 11,450 feet, 1 mile in, the trail levels and becomes gradual as the trees become sparser. Continue to follow your feet west for another 1.25 miles past willows, wildflowers, and glacial erratic

View from above Midway Tarn looking southeast across Independence Pass

boulders to reach the tarn and the spectacular views it offers of the high peaks. On a clear day, all of the highest Elk Range peaks are visible along the western horizon. Turn around and retrace your steps for a short day or a refreshing warm-up ahead of a bigger objective.

Overachievers can have a friend drop them off at the trailhead and follow the trail all the way north over Midway Pass (1.2 miles from the tarn) and down the Hunter Creek valley for a hefty 17.1 miles and 2,870 vertical gain (5,500 vertical descent). This makes for a very different day, and ventures through much more rugged, less frequented terrain.

MIDWAY TARN

N
Midway
12600
12400
12200
12000
11800
11600
Creek
3.2mi
Midway
Hunter-Fryingpan Wilde
11800
11600
11600
11400
11200
11000
Hunter-Fryingpan-Wilderness Area
White River National Forest
11400
11600
11200
11000
10800
10600
10400
Lost Man Loop
10800
10600
10400
10600
0.3mi
White River National Forest
Hunter-Fryingpan W
11000
11400
10800
Trailhead
CO 82
10600
Collegiate Peaks Wilderness
10800
11000
Road
11200
11600
11200
11800
11400
11400
MILES
0   0.1   0.2   0.3   0.4   0.5   0.6   0.7   0.8   0.9

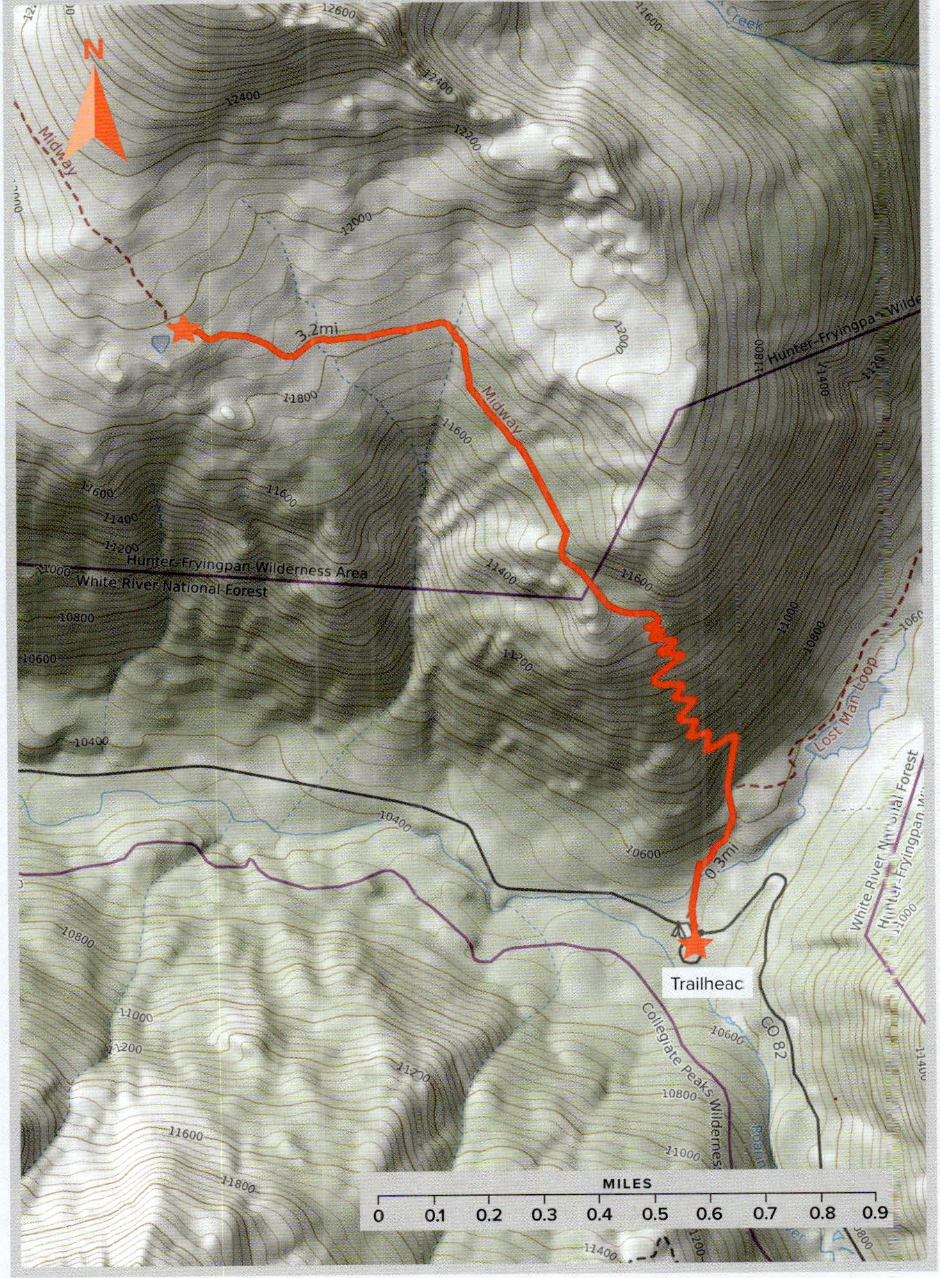

MIDWAY TARN WITH OPTIONAL EXTENSION

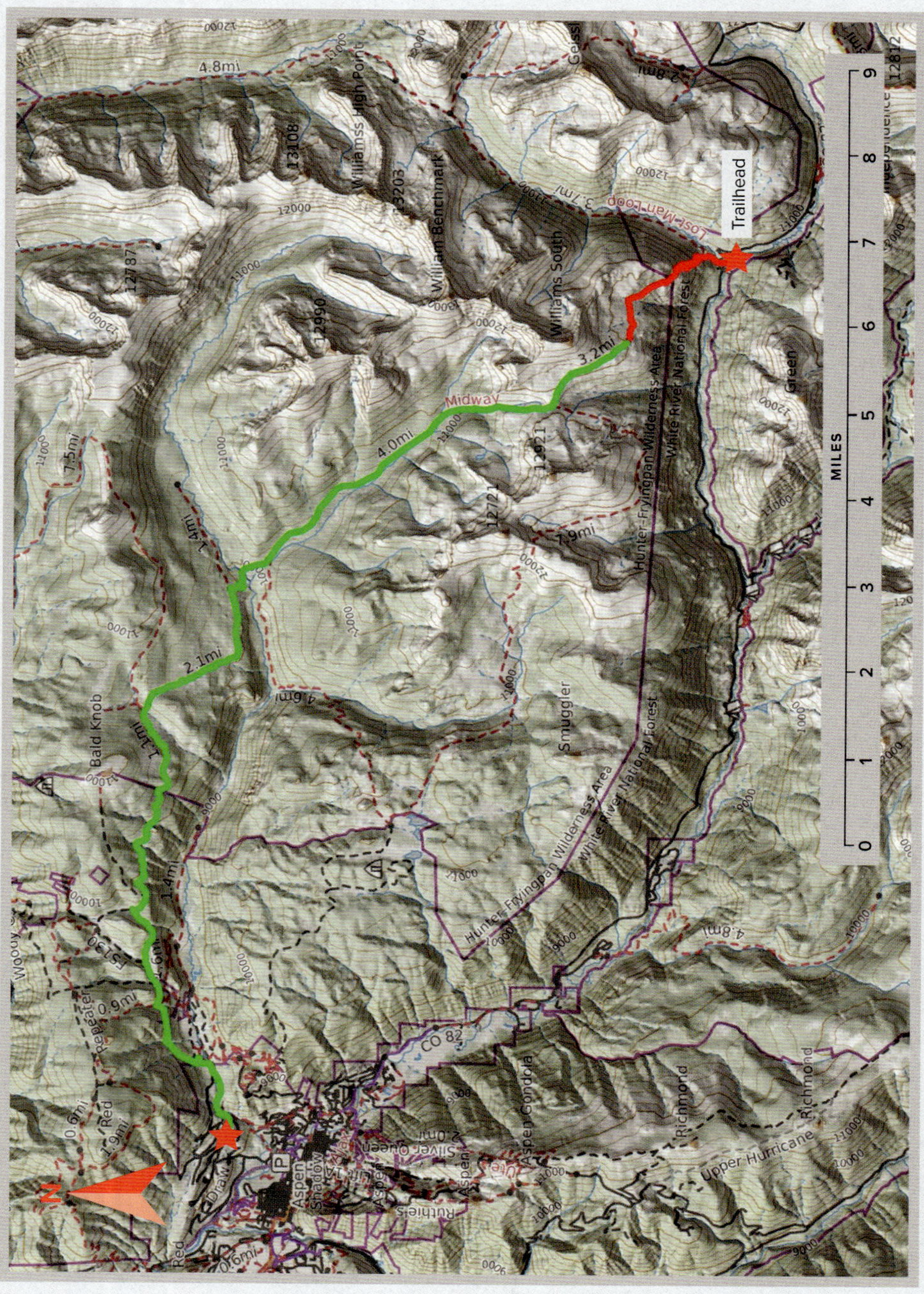

LOST MAN LOOP

15

Total Distance	8.8 miles (point-to-point)
Starting Elevation	11,510 feet
Ending Elevation	10,515 feet
High Point Elevation	12,795 feet
Total Elevation Gain	1,610 feet
Difficulty	■ Intermediate
Round-trip Time	1.5–2.5 hours
Runability	95%
Nearest Town	Aspen
Add-on	Retrace your steps for an out-and-back of 17.6 total miles and starting and finishing at a single trailhead.

COMMENT: This relatively undemanding point-to-point excursion is ideal for transitioning from shorter alpine runs. While a middle-distance route, it is mostly downhill and ideal for adjusting to higher elevations. If you want to make it more challenging, park only one vehicle at the lower trailhead and run it as an out-and-back for 17.6 miles.

Look back at Independence Lake before closing the final quarter mile up Lost Man Pass.

GETTING THERE: This route requires a car shuttle along CO Highway 82. With the help of a willing friend or running partner, leave a vehicle at the Lower Lost Man parking lot on the west side of Independence Pass, 13.4 miles east of Aspen. Drive a second vehicle 4.1 miles east up the pass to the Upper Lost Man/Independence Lake parking lot. Both dirt lots can be reached by bike, but be aware that Independence Pass does not have a bike lane, which makes for a narrow, at times treacherous squeeze with competing cars and overhanging rock faces. If you do ride, note that bikes will need to be locked on trees, as there are no bike racks. Note that dogs are allowed but must be on leash.

THE ROUTE: From the Upper Lost Man/Independence Lake parking lot, start up the trail alongside the creek and reach the Linkin Lake junction at not quite 0.2 mile. Stay right to continue ascending toward Independence Lake. These high-elevation miles pass quickly, and you'll reach the lake at 1.7 miles and 12,480 feet before you know it. Another 0.5 mile and 315 feet bring you to the top of Lost Man Pass.

Do a few jumping jacks here to loosen up your limbs for your rip-roaring 6.5-mile descent. Reach Lost Man Lake at mile 2.6 and 12,460 feet after a steep and rocky descent. Feel free to jump into this tranquil alpine lake if you can handle the

Independence Lake as viewed from above Lost Man Pass

chill. Afterward carry speed along a brief flat section before the trail curves westward into long alpine meadows.

Around mile 4.4, meet tree line again, though the conifers in this valley are widely spaced and stand in small clusters. Stay on this clear, well-trodden trail as you breeze past the junction at mile 4.8 (the alternative is a sharp right turn onto a thin, northbound trail). The Lost Man Trail curves southward, revealing the open view of 12,000- and 13,000-foot high points across the valley.

While this popular trail is exhilarating, with views sure to distract, be sure to pay careful attention to the several Lost Man Creek crossings in the second half of the run. The logs can be slick, especially early in the morning.

Most of the final 1.5 miles is pleasantly level and open as you pass through dewy willows and wildflowers. When you reach Lost Man Reservoir, you have only 0.6 mile to go. Push yourself to see how quickly you can close the final ground, racing past the Midway Trail turnoff at mile 8.5 and through the last cluster of trees to the parking lot.

LOST MAN LOOP

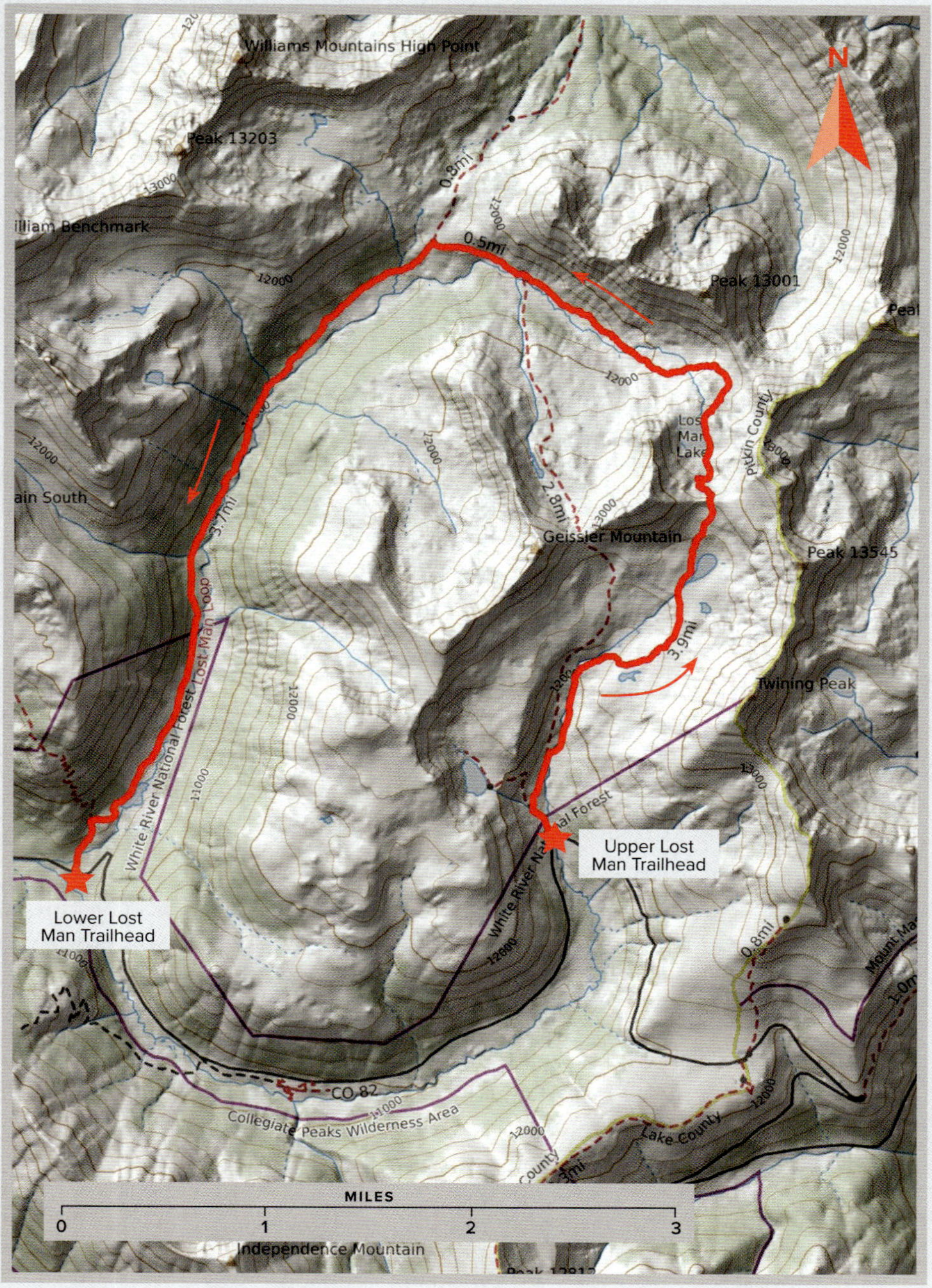

ASPEN HIGHLANDS

16

Total Distance	11 miles (out-and-back)
Starting Elevation	8,160 feet
High Point Elevation	12,360 feet
Total Elevation Gain	4,760 feet
Difficulty	◆ Difficult
Round-trip Time	2.5–4 hours
Runability	65%
Nearest Town	Aspen
Add-on	Five Trees Challenge

COMMENT: Highland Peak is best known as a ski season side-country destination for skilled skiers and snowboarders. Its dramatic north–south ridgeline, lift chair, prayer flag–adorned summit, and striking views of 14ers Pyramid Peak and the Maroon Bells make it worth a visit any time of year. It is generally runnable between early June and late October.

As you near the upper stretches of the road, the Maroon Bells become visible to the south.

GETTING THERE: From Aspen, head 0.4 mile west on CO Highway 82. At the roundabout, take the second right onto Maroon Creek Road. If running outside of the school year and starting your run with the Five Trees Challenge, take a left after 0.8 mile onto High School Road immediately after crossing under the pedestrian bridge. Take the next left to park in the Aspen High School parking lot and start your run from the Upper Moore ball field.

Otherwise, continue on Maroon Creek Road past the pedestrian bridge for an additional 0.6 mile. Take a left at the Aspen Highlands base area and park in the paid lot. Both the high school and ski area parking lots have places for cyclists to lock their bikes. Note that dogs are allowed but must be on leash.

THE ROUTE: Five Trees Challenge: Every year, the local teenage ski and snowboard athletes compete to see who can reach the top of the neighborhood Five Trees chairlift fastest on foot. This cross-country gauntlet covers 900 vertical feet in 1 mile. While some of it is along a dirt maintenance road, once on the ski mountain the most direct route is to bushwhack relatively straight up the 30–50 degree ski slope. The fastest teen athletes reach the top of the lift in 11–12 minutes each year, while the majority reach the top in 20–25 minutes. Are you masochistic enough to take it on?

If not subjecting yourself to the Five Trees Challenge, simply start at the Aspen Highlands base area and follow the main summer maintenance road. This meanders up the ski mountain for 5.9 miles, ascending 3,730 feet. It offers a behind-the-scenes look at the function of the ski resort, passing near each lift and restaurant on the mountain. Keep your eyes peeled for deer, bighorn sheep, and bears, all of which call the mountain home in dry months.

Pause on Loge Peak, overlooking the Highlands Ski Patrol hut, before continuing to the summit of Highland Peak.

The road ends between the Loge Peak and Deep Temerity ski lifts at 11,550 feet. Here you can take the 0.3-mile round-trip side jaunt to the Loge Peak summit (11,590 feet) above the ski patrol hut. Then return to the broad central ridge to continue following it south to the Highland Peak summit. Just 1 mile and 870 vertical feet remain. You are rapidly approaching tree line.

Only 0.3 mile after passing the top of the ski lifts, the wide ridge narrows to single-track with the famous Highland Bowl on your left (east) and dangerous backcountry terrain to your right (west). Navigate this narrowest section by staying on the thin path along the ski area boundary rope as you leave the last few lingering trees behind and ascend red, iron-rich talus. After this section, the steep finale of the ridge broadens again. Take advantage of the power-hiking pace to take photos so as to avoid distraction on your descent.

Finally, reach the summit at 12,360 feet. Pause to catch your breath and congratulate yourself; this route is one of the hardest of the lower-elevation routes in this book. You've earned these views. Carefully pick your way back down to the maintenance road, then let your legs carry you back to your starting point.

ASPEN HIGHLANDS

CAPITOL LAKE

17

Total Distance	12.6 miles (out-and-back)
Starting Elevation	9,463 feet
High Point Elevation	11,600 feet
Total Elevation Gain	2,600 feet
Difficulty	■ Intermediate
Round-trip Time	2–3 hours
Runability	95%
Nearest Town	Basalt

COMMENT: The valley that leads up to the base of one of Colorado's most notorious 14,000-foot peaks, Capitol Peak, bears a striking resemblance to the central Alps. If you're looking for particularly dramatic views, rolling trails through wildflower meadows, and encounters of the bovine kind, this is the run for you.

GETTING THERE: Turn off of CO Highway 82 at the Old Snowmass Conoco onto Snowmass Creek Road. Follow this for 1.8 miles to a T, then take a right and an

immediate slight left onto Capitol Creek Road (CO Highway 9). Shortly after the road turns to dirt (another 6.4 miles), you'll reach the Upper Capitol Lake Trailhead. A 4WD car with at least 7 inches of clearance and a shorter wheelbase is preferable. If driving a 2WD vehicle, park in the lower lot and expect an additional 4 miles round-trip and 980 feet vert for your run. While a mountain bike can reach the upper trail-head, options for stowing are limited to aspen trees, and the road is narrow and steep. Note that dogs are allowed but must be on leash.

THE ROUTE: Among Colorado's 14,000-foot peaks, Capitol is distinct. The gray granite peak is one of the most difficult and dangerous to summit. The approach to its base is particularly beautiful, with views of the mountain's precipitous north-northwest face from the majority of the trail, which pushes through aspen groves, high-altitude cattle grazing, wildflower meadows bursting with color, and patches of needle-carpeted, coniferous forest.

If starting from the lower trailhead, run up Capitol Creek Road, following it 2 miles to the upper trailhead, an uneven parking lot nestled among aspen groves and yielding the first haunting views of the treacherous peak. The road is popular and dusty, so runners may find a buff or other face covering helpful for this section.

At the upper parking lot, locate the signed trail at the southwest end of the lot. This is the Capitol Ditch Trail, and it will both allow you to get a true running warm-up to start, as well as save you a steep ascent at the end of your run. Enjoy the rolling track for these early miles through dappled aspen forest. Keep your feet light and an eye out for cows, which graze in this area during the summer months. When you exit the forest into your first meadow at 2.7 miles, pause for a photo of the imposing peak face and enjoy the exciting half-mile descent to the creek.

While shallow here, the creek is usually too wide to attempt a jump. If you have sensitive feet, you may prefer to change into a pair of dry socks shortly after the creek crossing. Continue southeast into a small section of coniferous forest, where you will join the Capitol Creek Valley Trail (as of 2022, this trail junction was not signed). The remaining 3 miles play peekaboo between patches of conifers and lush wildflower meadows. Enjoy the springy forest trail beneath your feet and

Descending to cross the creek

Capitol Lake and Capitol Peak in evening light

breathe deeply; the steepest ascent comes at mile 5.1 (10,800 feet) before relenting to a gradual rolling ascent again.

At 6 miles, emerge into the shadow of Capitol Peak. Dispersed campsites lie to your west, nestled in the remaining trees tenacious enough to hang on at this elevation. In this last 0.25 mile, pick your way to the lakeside with high feet on the musical talus. In addition to the imposing mountain to your immediate southeast, enjoy the view south toward Avalanche Basin and the rippling ridgeline of the seldom-visited 12,000-foot high points to your west and northwest. The majority of your descent is a gradual and joyful downhill, with just two brief climbs following the creek crossing as you reenter the aspen groves.

If you choose to do this run early or late in the day, you will feel the glacial echoes at Capitol Lake, the shaded icy-blue water nestled below the wall of grayish-white granite. The mellow trail gains a mere 2,600 feet over 6.3 miles.

Most of the Capitol Creek valley allows local landowners to graze cattle in the summer and autumn months. Be aware and conscientious of the livestock, especially if you are running with a canine companion.

CAPITOL LAKE

ELECTRIC PASS PEAK AND LEAHY PEAK

18

Total Distance	12 miles (out-and-back)
Starting Elevation	9,880 feet
High Point Elevation	13,640 feet
Total Elevation Gain	4,100 feet
Difficulty	■ Intermediate
Round-trip Time	2.5–4 hours
Runability	70%
Nearest Town	Aspen

COMMENT: Cathedral Basin, in the heart of the eastern Elk Range, inspires reverence in visitors. It features a glittering teal lake popular with fishermen, a ring of 13,000-foot peaks, a riot of colorful geological features, and sprawling wildflower meadows. The summits of this basin offer views of both the highest-elevation Elk peaks and of surrounding valleys, the Conundrum and Roaring Fork valleys in particular.

Electric Pass Peak as you ascend the upper Cathedral Basin

Castle and Cathedral Peaks to the north from the summit of Electric Pass Peak

GETTING THERE: Drive 0.5 mile west of Aspen on CO Highway 82 to the round-about. Go around the roundabout and turn right onto Castle Creek Road. Drive 12.2 miles. Watch for a dirt road on the right-hand side (west) 0.9 mile past Ashcroft Ghost Town. Turn right onto the dirt road and drive 0.5 mile to the Cathedral Lake Trailhead. 4WD and 7+ inches of vehicle clearance is helpful.

This is a very popular trailhead with a small dirt parking lot, so it is recommended that runners arrive either early in the morning or, if weather permits, late in the afternoon. Dogs are permitted on leash. Parking is free. The trail is generally fully clear of snow mid-June through mid-October, but during heavy snow years it may not clear until early July, and early autumn storms can obstruct the upper sections of trail.

THE ROUTE: This route serves up a variety of terrain, from meandering aspen forests along the creek to red Elk Range talus fields to a set of eleven punishingly steep switchbacks. From the clear parking lot trailhead sign, the first 0.75 mile travels through aspen groves before shifting to a mix of arid coniferous forest and open talus terrain for the next 1.75 miles.

Here you will encounter a series of eight steep switchbacks that serve as a gateway to the upper basin, gaining nearly 200 feet in less than 0.1 mile. This is the steepest section of the entire route. It is an excellent section to power hike before pausing in the trees for a snack and swig of water.

Within 0.1 mile of the topmost switchback, you will encounter a trail split. The right-hand trail continues into the upper basin toward Electric Pass Peak. The option straight ahead is a 0.3-mile (each way) detour to Cathedral Lake. Unless you are in need of a water refill, save that for later and take the right turn (west) and head upward. The next 0.25 mile and 215 vertical feet carry you above tree line which will provide your first real glimpse of the intimidating Cathedral ridgeline and an opportunity to evaluate the sky for any approaching weather. The iron rock of this basin attracts electrical charge from passing storms; if skies are ominous, cutting your run short is advisable.

Once in the upper basin, near and beyond Cathedral Lake, the route snakes through stunning south-facing alpine meadows that explode with wildflowers from June through September. Directly west of the single-track is the massive rock glacier that has been steadily accumulating from erosion of the Cathedral ridgeline for centuries. This runnable 2 miles of terrain climbs up to the ridge above to 13,000 feet.

Many hikers choose to stop at the saddle of Electric Pass Peak, which sits at 13,180 feet, a half mile from the summit. The final half mile is more technical but does not exceed Class 2, passing beyond tundra into talus steps that traverse the peak's south face. High and energetic feet are advisable.

As you near the yellow-red summit of Electric Pass Peak, so named for its iron rich and lightning-rod geology, the horizon opens up. This rewards the viewer with the turquoise gem of Cathedral Lake in a valley that combines the paradisiacal meadows with the foreboding rock glaciers seeping outward from the jagged Cathedral Peak ridgeline.

From the top of Electric Pass Peak, it is 0.3 mile back to the ridge saddle if you follow the ridge directly. Another 0.6 mile east-southeast along the alpine ridge crest takes you to the summit of Leahy Peak. This section is not on maintained trail, so step mindfully. This mellow second peak is worth the effort, with contrasting views of gentle alpine meadows to your right and a steep drop toward the Castle Creek Valley to your left. Like the first summit, you will be treated to a ringing vista of the Elk high peaks and the greater Roaring Fork Valley. The long Sawatch Range unfolds to the east.

From these high points, the return to the trailhead is an exhilarating, beautiful run.

Moss campion at 13,000 feet

The rugged spires of Cathedral Peak as seen while descending back toward Cathedral Lake

Cathedral Lake can provide a brisk and refreshing plunge on the way down. It is a popular picnic and fishing spot, so be respectful of other visitors should you choose to add it to your run.

Wildflowers along the route include Indian paintbrush, columbines, bluebells, the cheery yellow Old-Man-of-the-Mountains, and blue shades of alpine forget-me-nots. Pikas and ptarmigans are occasionally encountered along the highest 1,000 feet of the route.

Stay close to the top of the ridge as you frolic along the ridge to Leahy Peak.

ELECTRIC PASS PEAK AND LEAHY PEAK

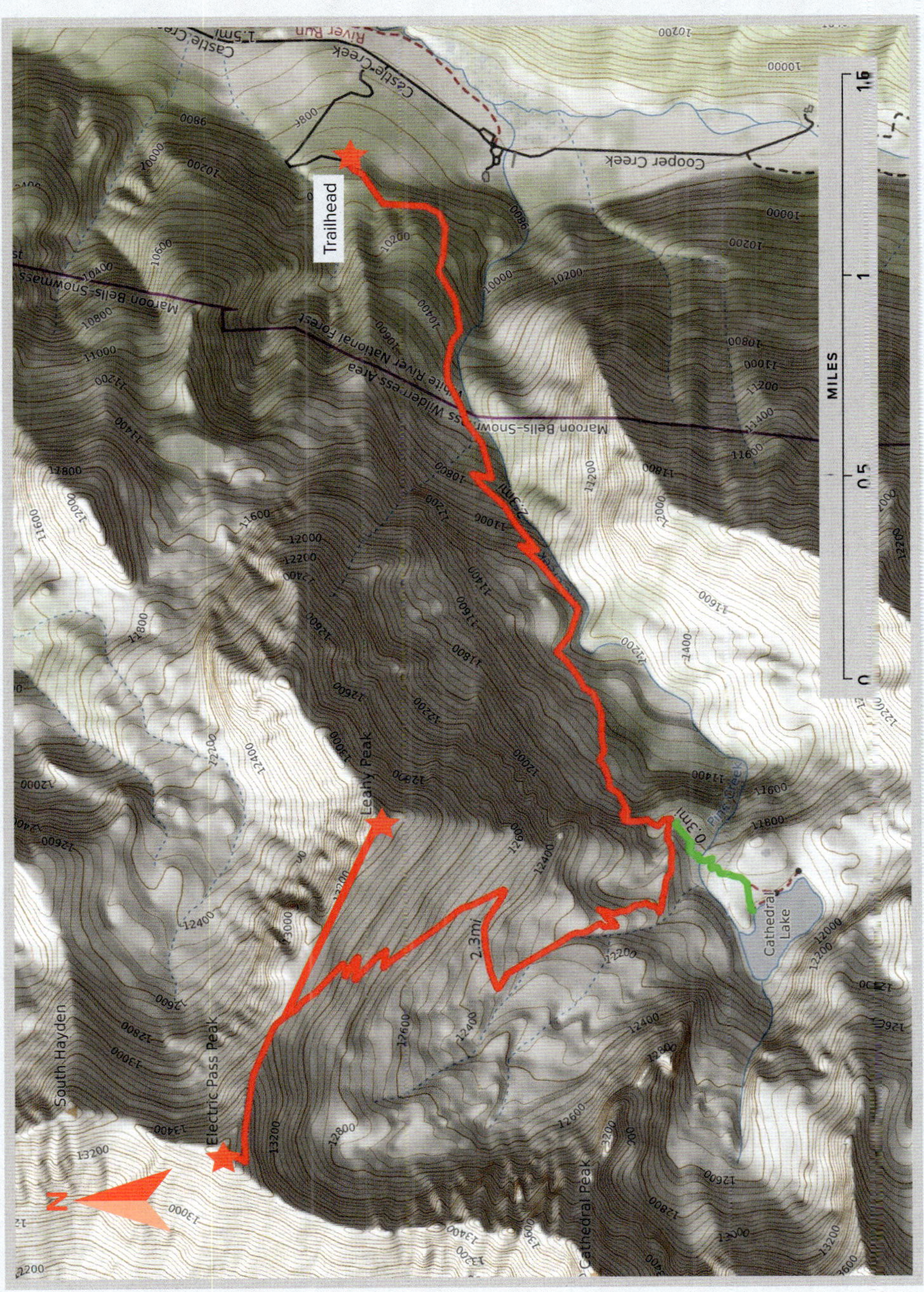

CASTLE PEAK

19

Total Distance	13.5 miles (out-and-back)
Starting Elevation	9,800 feet
High Point Elevation	14,260 feet
Total Elevation Gain	4,600 feet
Difficulty	◆◆ Most Difficult
Round-trip Time	2.5–4.5 hours
Runability	70%
Nearest Town	Aspen
Add-on	Conundrum Peak (14,060 feet)

COMMENT: Castle Peak is the highest and easternmost of the Elk 14ers, but also the lowest relative risk of the 14ers in this range. The backcountry road up into Montezuma Basin carries runners back through time, past abandoned mines, across creek beds, and up onto soaring purple ridges. Look closely and you might spot an ermine in the talus or a tenacious, periwinkle sky pilot blossom along the summit ridge.

Conundrum Peak as seen from the Castle summit ridge

Montezuma Basin, with the trail visible ascending from the upper basin to the summit ridge

GETTING THERE: Drive 0.5 mile west of Aspen on CO Highway 82 to the round-about. Go around the roundabout and turn right onto Castle Creek Road. Drive 12.5 miles to the end of the paved road. A wooden Forest Service sign marks the small dirt parking lot at the base of the dirt road that provides high-clearance 4WD access. Although dogs are permitted in this area, it is not recommended to take them on the upper sections of Castle Peak as the exposed terrain can make them a hazard to other travelers and themselves.

THE ROUTE: This classic run leaves the pavement and enters another world, delving through forest and up into the spires and parapets of Montezuma Basin. Much of the route is dirt mountain road, which makes the vertical gain much friendlier. There is a road split 2.9 miles up from the 2WD parking; be sure to take the right (west) fork to enter Montezuma Basin and head toward Castle Peak. The left (south) fork is a much rougher mountain road leading toward Pearl Pass.

Continue to jog or power hike up the road to the high 4WD parking lot at 12,800 feet. The slopes above you to your right (north) are spotted with mining ruins underneath the gendarmes of Malemute Peak. These include collapsed sheds as well as rusted cables, which add echoes of human infrastructure to the rugged ridgelines and watersheds around you. After gaining around 3,000 vertical feet over 5.5 miles, you reach the upper basin and transition to cairns and scree single-track.

In early to mid-summer, there will likely be remaining snowfields, and poles and microspikes come in handy here. If you do not encounter snow in this section of the basin, watch carefully for cairns along the left (east) side of the basin. These mark the faint trail that switchbacks up the side of the rock glacier from 12,800 to 13,350 feet (just under 0.4 mile). Step carefully, as parts of this section of trail have loose dirt that can make it easy to slip. With or without snow, power hiking suits this brief stretch well, which gains 1,500 feet in 0.8 mile between the 4-wheeling parking lot and the summit.

At 13,350 feet, reach a flatter section of the basin and turn left (east) to traverse upward and south toward the ridge crest. Upon gaining the ridge at 13,700 feet, it is prudent to keep pace at hiking speed as you'll be navigating thin, exposed trail on crumbling Elk shale. Sections of the trail on the ridge are clear, but there are a few slightly scrambly sections as well. If you are less familiar with routefinding on rock, take your time to carefully find stable steps. If you are using poles, you may want to put them away here in order to keep your hands free for stabilization.

In this last 0.25 mile, views of the other Elk 14ers open to your west, while verdant wild valleys stretch away to the southeast. The rock on this upper section of the ridge shows beautiful mineral tinges in the shale, from light turquoise (traces

Hikers navigating a technical and tricky section of the ridge. This requires scrambling with use of one or both hands.

Left: The view from below of the technical section (which is depicted from above on the previous page). Watch closely for foot- and handholds on your left and stay relatively close to the ridge crest. **Right:** A sky pilot blossom at 14,000 feet along the summit ridge

of copper) to a rich grayish purple, likely from iron and manganese. A close look also reveals tenacious microflora along the section of north-facing ridge, with the occasional sky pilot blossom among the largest plant growth. (Note: Exposure in this final section is some of the most extreme described in this guidebook if you have a fear of heights, you may choose not to run this route. While you can turn around at the top of the 4-wheeling road at 12,800 feet, the views to that point are much less spectacular than the final mile of the ascent.)

After summiting, maintain extra care on the first mile of descent. Once you reach the road, however, you can enjoy a pleasant, steady jog back down.

Conundrum Peak can be added to your route from the summit of Castle Peak, if desired. This will add an extra mile and 735 vertical feet to your day. Do not run the descent from Castle Peak northwest to the Conundrum saddle; this rock is very loose and an incautious step can result in a rolled ankle or worse. The thin trail that reascends to the Conundrum summit is firmer, but still requires close attention. The recognized summit of Conundrum is the northern of the two, just over 0.1 mile past the south summit.

If you add Conundrum Peak to your day and there is not snow to the Conundrum saddle at 13,800 feet, *do not* descend from the saddle, but instead reascend Castle Peak and descend via the described route. With snow, descending from the Conundrum saddle can be a pleasant glissade. Without snow, it is very loose Class 3 downclimbing that should not be attempted without a helmet.

CASTLE PEAK

Cooper Cr
Cooper Cr
11200
10800
10600
10000
Trailhead
Cooper Creek
10600
10200
10400
10000
Pine Creek
White River National
Maroon Bells-Snowmass Wilderness A
White River National Forest
10200
10000
10200
10400
10600
10200
12200
11400
10800
11000
11200
2.7mi
12200
12400
12600
12000
12400
11400
11800
12000
2.3mi
Pine Creek
Cathedral Lake
Malamute Peak
12800
12600
12400
12000
White River National Forest
12000
12200
12400
12800
13000
Cathedral Peak
13200
12800
12600
13000
12400
12600
12200
12200
12400
13000
13200
Conundrum Peak
South Conundrum Peak
Castle Peak
0.5mi
0.6mi
1800
Castle Peak-West Peak
Pitkin Conundrum
13400
13600
13200
13400
13200
Creek
11800
11600
11400
11200
11800
12000
12200
12400
12600
12800
13200
MILES
0
1
2
3
N

MOUNT SOPRIS

20

Total Distance	13.5 miles (out-and-back)
Starting Elevation	8,655 feet
High Point Elevation	12,966 feet
Total Elevation Gain	4,665 feet
Difficulty	◆◆ Most Difficult
Round-trip Time	3.5–5 hours
Runability	70%
Nearest Towns	Basalt/Carbondale
Add-on	West Sopris (12,966 feet)

COMMENT: This Elk Range running classic offers a refreshing variety of terrain. From forested single-track to high-alpine ridge running, you'll encounter views of deep, green valleys and high, dramatic peaks. This route packs a punch of vertical gain into moderate mileage.

The Sopris massif due south 2 miles into your approach

GETTING THERE: From Basalt, head west on CO Highway 82 for 1.5 miles. Turn left (south) onto Emma Road, then turn immediately left again to follow Sopris Creek Road for 1.1 miles. Turn right onto West Sopris Creek Road and follow for 5.6 miles. At this point, the road turns to dirt. Just after the Crown Mountain Trailhead parking on the right, turn left at the Prince Creek Road intersection onto Dinkle Lake Road and follow it for 2 miles to the Mount Sopris Trailhead. Eight inches of clearance is essential for these 2 miles.

THE ROUTE: The first mile from the trailhead follows gentle switchbacks along broad, sandy, and rocky trail through mixed forest. The grade here is gentle enough to run if you feel energetic but can be taken at a power hike if you prefer a more gradual warm-up. At 9,150 feet, the trail flattens for 0.8 mile as it heads south. In this stretch, pass through a gate and enter a stretch of sagebrush and wildflowers.

Round a corner and come to a signed fork in the trail at the edge of aspen forest. The left trail goes to Hay Park; take the right and head west for 0.3 mile before the trail turns south again to enter the aspens. This next stretch of trail rolls as it meanders through the primarily deciduous forest. Wildlife such as foxes and deer are common sights in the early morning hours or close to twilight. After another 1.3 miles, come to the first of the Thomas Lakes as the forest becomes more coniferous.

Looking eastward across the Elk Range as you prepare to descend from the east summit

COLORADO ALPINE TRAIL RUNS

The second and largest lake is 0.2 mile away. The jade-colored water reflects the looming eastern summit and false summit of the mountain. The broad stony shore of this lake is a popular picnic spot for hikers. You may want to pick out where along the lake shore you'd like to pause for a refreshing dip on your descent.

At 4.2 miles total and 10,330 feet, pass the third and final lake. From here, the trail begins steadily climbing. This is the actual flank of the mountain. Over the next 1.6 miles, gain 1,300 vertical feet as the coniferous forest thins and other Elk Range peaks become visible to your southeast. Fearsome 14ers Capitol Peak and Snowmass Mountain loom behind a geographical feature known among local runners as Dream Ridge, which stretches 6.5 miles from the eastern shoulder of Sopris all the way to the upper Capitol Creek valley. That backcountry route is visible to the east for most of your Sopris run.

Once atop Sopris's northeast ridge, continue up this more eroded section of trail through stunted high-elevation spruce. Reach the last of the dwarfish and gnarled krummholz at around 5.5 miles and 11,700 feet, just before a narrow section of the ridge. The next 0.6 mile and 700 vertical feet of the route are the most precarious, so exercise caution along the thin trail. While the technicality does not exceed Class 2, this stretch of trail crosses loose scree with slope angles as high as 40 degrees, so take care to stay on the trail and choose solid foot placements. Those uncomfortable with exposure may prefer to set their turnaround point before starting this section.

The second and largest of Thomas Lakes, with the summit ridge looming beyond

At 6 miles, pass over the top of the false summit, and regain more stable talus and the summit ridge at 6.1 miles and 12,333 feet. A mere 0.6 mile remain to the east summit at 12,966 feet. This final stretch is classic alpine running, with talus single-track along a ridge that slopes gently south and drops sharply to the north.

Ascending the summit ridge after navigating past the false summit.

For most of the summer, thin remnants of snow cornice remain along the north side of the ridge. Reach the summit and take in the spectacular 360-degree views of the Roaring Fork and Crystal River Valleys before turning to descend.

If you would like to extend your run, you can continue west along the ridge crest for 0.7 mile to reach the twin western summit of Sopris. This will add a total of 1.4 miles and 600 feet vertical gain to your day. While a relatively short distance, this should only be included with excellent weather, as there is no alternative route back to the trailhead from the western summit.

MOUNT SOPRIS

SNOWMASS THREE PASS LOOP

21

Total Distance	23 miles (loop)
Starting Elevation	8,420 feet
High Point Elevation	12,690 feet
Total Elevation Gain	5,930 feet
Difficulty	◆◆ Most Difficult
Round-trip Time	4.5–8 hours
Runability	80%
Nearest Town	Snowmass

COMMENT: The lesser-known sibling to the Four Pass Loop (p. 106), this route ascends the less-trafficked East Snowmass valley below 13,000-foot ridges before knocking out all three passes in less than 4 miles of the route. The long descent down the West Snowmass valley includes a visit to Snowmass Lake and a wide variety of trail technicality to keep the downhill interesting. Clockwise directions are given here, but the route can be run in either direction.

GETTING THERE: From CO Highway 82, turn southwest at the Old Snowmass stoplight and Conoco. Follow this road 1.8 miles to the T intersection. Take a left and follow it 9.2 miles to another intersection, then take a right and continue 0.4 mile to the parking lot. A vehicle with 4WD is helpful in the final mile.

Left: Reach the unnamed pass at 7.2 miles, and bask in the view of Pyramid Peak to the south as you start your first descent. **Right:** After an exhilarating descent of Willow Pass, continue heading due south toward the looming Maroon Bells. The next turn (a right) will sneak up after you reenter willows.

THE ROUTE: From the West Snowmass Creek lot, head due north along the road for 0.1 mile to the East Snowmass Creek Trailhead on the right-hand (east) side of the road. Get ready to gain; the first 0.7 mile carries you up 540 vertical feet. At 1.2 miles, take a right at a trail junction to stay on the East Snowmass Creek Trail. Continue through these high conifers along soft, needle-padded trail.

The next section comes as the forest transitions to more aspens in terrain that has been molded by avalanches over the years. Keep a steady but measured warm-up pace as the trail curves to the south at mile 2.4 and you reach the mouth of the East Snowmass Creek valley. Along the next 2.3 miles, mind the foliage along the trail; one of the many plants in the mix is stinging nettle, which causes itching and burning if it brushes bare skin. (Should you accidentally touch any nettles, do not rub or scratch, but gently rinse with water at the next stream you cross.)

At 4.7 miles, the trail crosses yet another avalanche path regrowing with willows and aspens into a stand of conifers. A few more such crossings remain, but you have only vertical feet left to tree line and 2.5 miles left to the top of the first pass. At the top of this unnamed pass, the highest point of the route, take a moment to breathe, eat, drink, and snap photos of the views. You have a particularly excellent view of 14er Pyramid Peak looming behind Willow Lake.

Descend for 1 mile and reach a brief trail junction. Take a right to head toward Willow Pass instead of Willow Lake. A mellow climb brings you to the top of the pass at 8.9 miles and 12,536 feet, which includes an arresting view of 14er North Maroon Peak over the Buckskin valley. This next descent is the steepest of the loop, dropping 250 feet in just 0.2 mile.

At 8.1 miles, take a right at the signpost to head toward Willow Pass rather than Willow Lake.

Shortly before you reach the Buckskin trail junction, cross a small creek, which is an opportunity to fill and treat a water bottle if needed. At the junction at 9.8 miles, turn right (west) and settle into a steady power hike to ascend your third and final pass. Crest Buckskin Pass at 10.7 miles. Pause for another short break to marvel at the many soaring peaks.

Follow the westward switchbacks down off of Buckskin Pass and meet tree line again at 12 miles. This creek crossing is another good opportunity for filling bottles if needed. Then descend another 1.3 miles down steep, winding trail to your largest water crossing at mile 13.3 and 10,843 feet. Face the last significant aspect of the day, 240 feet in 0.8 mile, before resuming a downhill trend.

At mile 14.6, take a sharp right at the trail intersection to contour around the north end of Snowmass Lake and meet the West Snowmass Trail. Just 8.4 northward-bound miles remain; it's all downhill from here.

Pause to take in the views at Snowmass Lake before continuing your descent.

SNOWMASS THREE PASS LOOP

FOUR PASS LOOP

22

Total Distance	28 miles (loop)
Starting Elevation	9,576 feet
High Point Elevation	12,454 feet
Total Elevation Gain	7,265 feet
Difficulty	◆◆ Most Difficult
Round-trip Time	5–10 hours
Runability	75%
Nearest Town	Aspen

COMMENT: Possibly the most famous of Elk Range alpine runs, the Four Pass Loop is popular among hikers, runners, and backpackers for its idyllic views of iconic red peaks, Snowmass Lake's picturesque shores, its quarto of unique passes, and the wildflowers and waterfalls you'll pass along the way. A jaunt here is sure to leave your body tired and your soul refreshed. Make sure to bring ample calories, water treatment, and some kind of camera.

A dawn start yields some spectacular views of the Maroon Bells, especially in midsummer.

The Snowmass and Capitol massif looms large to the west until you descend back below tree line.

GETTING THERE: Reservations are required to access Maroon Lake. I recommend obtaining a reservation for your vehicle; there is a shuttle bus from Aspen Highlands; however, it does not start early enough for the preferable run start time (4:30–6 a.m.). Reservations cost $10 per vehicle and are made online at aspenchamber.org. When making your reservation, you will choose Day Visit or 24 hour, depending on how fast you plan to run. Drop-offs at the lake are allowed between 6 and 8 a.m. without a parking reservation. Runners who choose this option are advised to buy a one-way bus ticket for their return trip from Maroon Lake to Aspen Highlands. Maroon Lake parking is 9.4 miles up Maroon Creek Road from the Aspen roundabout.

THE ROUTE: At Maroon Lake, check that you have adequate layers, water treatment, and plenty of calories. A significant adventure lies ahead of you. The Four Pass Loop can be run in either direction; many prefer counterclockwise, as it allows you to finish with a more gradual descent after the fourth pass. Those instructions are provided here.

Head south on Crater Lake Trail, keeping a wary eye out for local moose. At 1.7 miles, reach the fork for Buckskin Pass; take this sharp right and quickly shift into a steady power hike. This trail climbs westward via switchbacks and soon leaves tree line. If you look back, you'll see the massive silhouette of 14er Pyramid Peak dominating your view to the east.

Continue at a measured pace, taking a left at the trail fork at 3.8 miles, then rapidly close the remaining distance to the top of Buckskin Pass. If you start early enough, you can hit this 12,450-foot, 4.8-mile point as sunrise breaks over the Pyramid ridge to the east and alpenglow decorates the Snowmass massif to the west.

The views south across the Raggeds Wilderness from Trail Rider Pass are breathtaking.

Keep high feet as you start your first descent of the day. Meet tree line again at 6.3 miles and 11,600 feet. If you need to refill water, this creek crossing is a good spot for it. Then continue this playful, technical descent toward Snowmass Lake. After crossing a tributary creek, ascend briefly again for 200 vertical feet, then reach a trail junction approaching the shores of the lake at mile 8.7. Take a hard left (south) and follow the trail as it traverses a scree slope above the lake, bypassing the crowded camping areas.

Especially early in the summer, you can expect to encounter some snowfields as you move back above tree line approaching Trail Rider Pass on these north-facing slopes. Soon enough, reach the top of this rugged north–south pass at 11 miles and 12,400 feet. The formidable 13er Snowmass Peak looms threateningly to your immediate west.

Start your second descent and head south into the upper Geneva valley. At 12 miles, there are tarns and creeks that are good places to fill and treat water if needed. Then continue south-southeast toward your most technical descent of the route, staying left at trail junctions. Confidence, momentum, and nimble feet are extremely helpful as you negotiate trail down steep switchbacks and sidehill traversing through aspen forest.

At mile 13.8 and 10,280 feet, now heading southeast, start the long and deceptive false flat ascent through the Fravert Basin. When you spot the thundering North Fork waterfall, you're getting close to the third pass, but not as close as you might hope. Another 2.3 miles remain to pass back above tree line, and then another 1.2 miles yet to reach the top of the 12,340-foot pass. Distract yourself by taking in the stunning and less famous southwest perspective of the Maroon Bells.

The loneliest of the passes, Frigid Air is a welcome high point after long valley miles and a gradual ascent.

The top of Frigid Air Pass marks 18.7 miles, where you are 68 percent done with the loop. One more significant climb remains. Descend southeastward into Purity Basin, again keeping left at trail junctions. Reach a low point of 11,725 feet before starting your final climb up West Maroon Pass. At the top, 12,460 feet and 21.2 miles, take a break to fuel, hydrate, and congratulate yourself in this dramatic setting of red rock.

Shake your legs out and tackle the 6.5-mile descent back to Maroon Lake. Sections of the trail near Crater Lake are nearly flat, so some caffeine at the top of the pass may help you push through these miles to the last downhill mile between Crater and Maroon Lakes. You just conquered an iconic American alpine run. Celebrate by lying down on the sidewalk with your feet up on the wooden fence to let some of that lactic acid drain out of your legs.

FOUR PASS LOOP

SAN JUAN RANGE

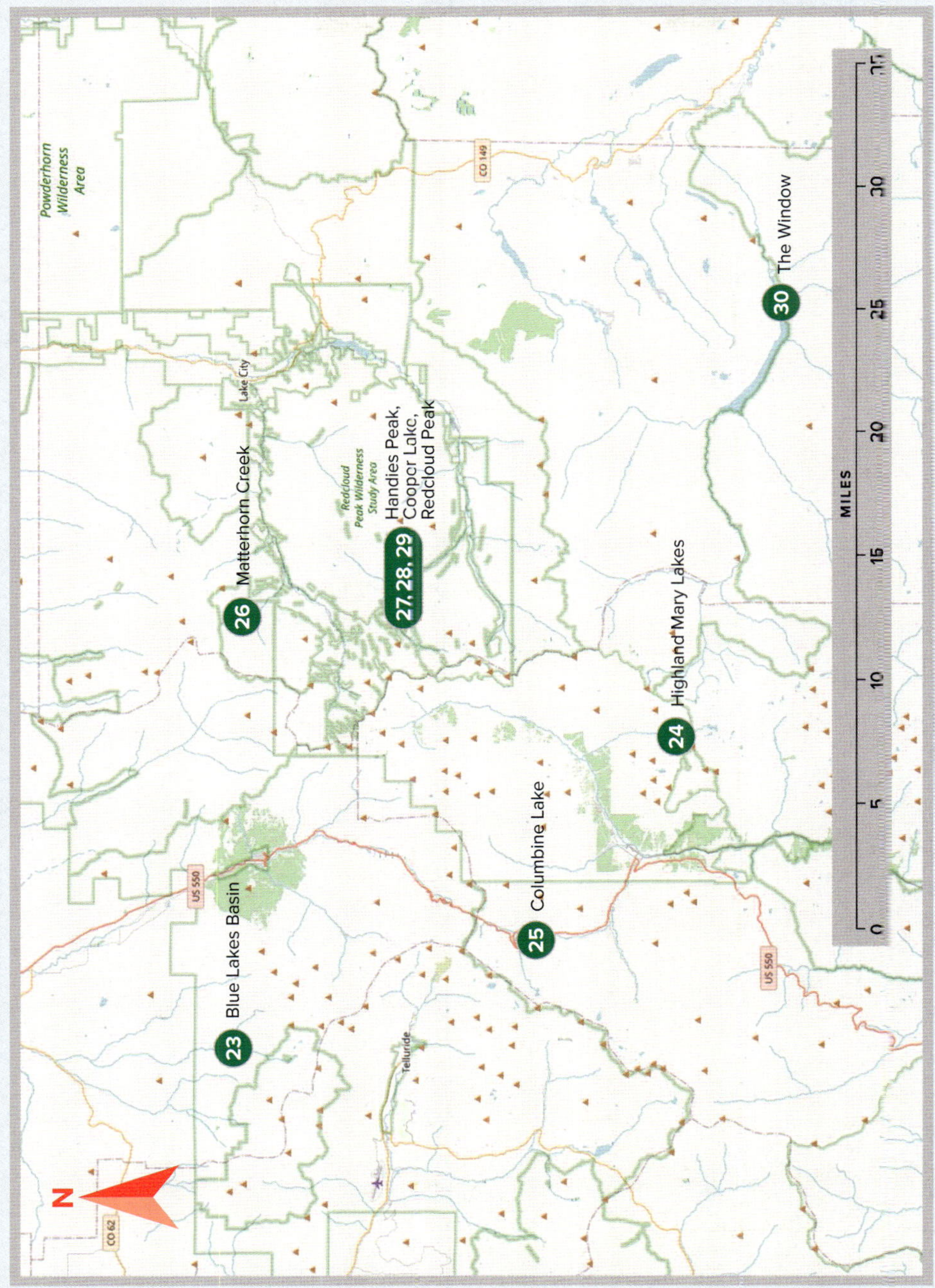

BLUE LAKES BASIN

23

Total Distance	8.4 miles (out-and-back)
Starting Elevation	9,355 feet
High Point Elevation	11,760 feet
Total Elevation Gain	2,900 feet
Difficulty	■ Intermediate
Round-trip Time	1.5–2.5 hours
Runability	75%
Nearest Town	Ridgway
Add-on	Yankee Boy Basin

COMMENT: The Blue Lakes, nestled just west of the iconic Mount Sneffels, are one of the many striking landscape features that inspire the region's nickname, "Switzerland of America." These tiered glacial gems are popular with backpackers, fishermen, photographers, and runners. In midsummer, you can expect this area to be a busy

The trail just below tree line and Middle Blue Lake

destination. If you are hoping to avoid crowds, plan your excursion for early summer, late autumn, or the beginning or end of a day.

GETTING THERE: Reach Ridgway via US Highway 550. Turn west onto CO Highway 62 and follow it for 4.8 miles. You will reach a turnoff onto dirt road CR 7. At least 7 inches of clearance, 4WD, and experience on rocky roads is preferable. Stay on CR 7; do not take any of the turns off of this main road. After 7.5 miles, you will start to see camping spaces, followed by the Blue Lakes Trailhead parking lot at mile 8.9.

THE ROUTE: From the trailhead, the legs warm up quickly, as the single-track through old growth conifer forest climbs steadily, alternating between switchbacks, traverses, and rolling sections in the tallest stands of trees. The trail underfoot varies from spongy humus to dusty switchbacks, and plenty of roots keep things exciting. Here and there, it is possible to glimpse the north and west ridges of Sneffels looming high to your left.

The grade relaxes as you approach the first lake at 3.1 miles in; though it may be tempting to pause among the campsites and crowds to admire the mineral-rich cyan water, resist. Better views lie ahead. Instead, cross the creek and tackle the next upward plunge of trail, as the dirt beneath your feet shifts from the spongy

As you pass middle Blue Lake, the saddle between Mount Sneffels and Dallas Peak starts coming into view.

dark humus of the forest floor to the dry, sunbaked grit of exposed earth close to tree line. As you navigate up a rib of steeper terrain, the valley floor recedes dramatically. At 3.7 miles, after a few thin, talusy stream crossings, the shining gem of water far below will insist upon attention. Don't forget to look up and marvel at the jagged peaks ringing this valley, with cirques and steppes carved out by glaciers long since gone.

Two more lakes lie ahead as you leave the last few stands of spruce and pine behind around 3.9 miles. Above tree line, the trail grows tamer again, weaving sedately around the second lake and meandering toward the saddle of the pass, which crumbles like so many Greek ruins at the junction of the Sneffels and Dallas ridgelines. The third lake hides not far below the pass, 4.2 miles and 2,900 vertical feet above the trailhead.

If the skies look friendly, you could head over into Yankee Boy Basin for a longer day. The 0.9-mile ascent from the third lake to the Sneffels–Dallas saddle (the gateway to Yankee Boy Basin) involves a hefty 1,240 feet of additional vertical gain. Or simply relish these soaring views, listen for pika chirps, and then ride your legs 4.2 miles back down the single-track roller coaster to the trailhead.

BLUE LAKES BASIN

HIGHLAND MARY LAKES

24

Total Distance	5 miles (out-and-back)
Starting Elevation	10,780 feet
High Point Elevation	12,120 feet
Total Elevation Gain	1,340 feet
Difficulty	● Beginner
Round-trip Time	1.25–2.5 hours
Runability	95%
Nearest Town	Silverton
Add-on	Unnamed 13,020′ or Peak 12,905′

COMMENT: A collection of alpine lakes that is most visited by Colorado Trail thru-hikers, this basin of hidden gems offers playful trail, gently rolling terrain, countless waterfalls, and breathtaking views of the Grenadier and Needle subranges.

GETTING THERE: From Silverton, head east through town and turn south (right) onto CO Highway 110/2. This road continues up toward Engineer and Cinnamon Passes. At 4.1 miles up, turn west (right) onto CR 4 toward Stony Pass. CR 4 curves gradually south along Cunningham Creek. Most vehicles with 4WD and 6–7 inches of clearance will be able to make it to the free signed camping in the basin, 3.3 miles from the Stony Pass turn.

High-clearance vehicles will be able to reach the upper trailhead 1.3 miles beyond the camping spaces. Do not attempt to drive to the upper trailhead without a well-equipped, high-clearance 4WD vehicle. There is one creek crossing shortly before the upper parking.

THE ROUTE: From the upper Highland Mary Lakes parking lot, follow the Highland Mary Lake Trail roughly south and upward. The first 1.2 miles treat you to countless waterfalls alongside the trail, ranging in size from delicate ribbons to broad cascades of water launching over boulders. The vertical gain in this section is 900 feet, steep enough that you may choose to power hike initially.

At 1.9 miles from the trailhead, you will reach the first lake and upper basin. This is quite close to tree line at 12,100 feet, so the remaining conifers are few and far between. The vertical gain relaxes here, as the trail navigates through low willows and along the perimeter of the many lakes. Especially in early summer, this is an excellent vantage point for wildflower photos.

Be sure to take in the wildflowers in the basin.

It is another 0.6 mile between the two largest lakes to the end of the primary route and well-established trail. However, there are multiple options for increasing your run, should you wish to do more than 5 miles round-trip.

You can continue to follow the trail 0.5 mile to the southern rim of the basin. Here, turn right off of the trail and bushwhack your way southwest along the top of a gentle ridgeline, crossing an unnamed 13,020-foot high point. After an additional 1.5 miles, you'll find yourself atop the far point of the ridge at 12,943 feet. From this point you will have an astonishing view of the dramatic Grenadier Range to the south, with Vestal and Arrow Peaks rising with the abrupt insistence of a 1980s pop hit in the foreground. These rugged views are complemented by the gently rolling alpine meadows and sapphire lakes of the basin that stretches to the north.

Another alternative is to head due east (turning left) for 0.8 mile from the largest of the Highland Mary Lakes, ascending Peak 12,905′ along the eastern rim of the basin. After taking in the views, drop to the Continental Divide Trail and follow it north for 1.2 miles, then take a left at the trail fork and descend 1.8 exhilarating miles back to the Highland Mary Lake Trailhead to make your outing a 6.7-mile loop.

HIGHLAND MARY LAKES

COLUMBINE LAKE

25

Total Distance	5.7 miles (out-and-back)
Starting Elevation	10,285 feet
High Point Elevation	12,720 feet
Total Elevation Gain	2,625 feet
Difficulty	■ Intermediate
Round-trip Time	1–1.5 hours
Runability	75%
Nearest Town	Silverton/Ouray

COMMENT: Columbine Lake is one of the shining gems of the San Juans. This looming glacial basin is tucked away above the Million Dollar Highway and Red Mountain Pass, in the midst of several unassuming 13,000-foot peaks that receive less attention than the region's 14ers.

GETTING THERE: Take Red Mountain Pass (US Highway 550) between Ouray and Silverton. At 1 mile south of the Mill Creek hairpin corner, look out for a subtle dirt road turnoff (Forest Road 820) on the west side of the road. There is sufficient

After exiting tree line, continue following the trail west toward the next set of switchbacks.

This brief exposed traverse takes you over a shoulder into Columbine Basin.

shoulder for lower-clearance vehicles to park along the side of this dirt road. High-clearance vehicles can cross the creek and follow the road for 0.75 mile to the base of the trail's switchbacks. There is not a specific parking lot; park along the shoulder of the road, leaving room for other vehicles to drive past.

THE ROUTE: The trail is not marked and begins with an abrupt turn up into the trees from the road. This jaunt starts with an energetic power hike up sixteen switchbacks that get you close to tree line. After the switchbacks, 1.3 miles in and 1,000 feet gained already, the grade relaxes considerably as the trail threads through open mixed forest and into a broad, open alpine basin.

The terrain may trick you into thinking the lake is near, but there is still plenty of fun trail left. A few additional switchbacks above a small plateau lead to a slight saddle to cross into the Columbine basin. At this saddle, there is the option to take a short 0.2-mile detour east to a 12,682-foot high point with more dramatic views of peaks across the valley. Note that in early summer, the sections of this trail above tree line can have multiple lingering snowdrifts due to the northeast aspects. While quite refreshing, this can also mean that you may want to have microspikes with you for traction.

As you continue to follow the trail west, the views are more rugged, with red and white high points eroding with infinitesimal slowness. Finally, in the upper

You may choose to take the mini detour to the top of the high point just off-trail for the viewpoint of the surrounding San Juan peaks.

belly of the basin, 2.9 miles and 12,720 feet in elevation, you reach the deep blue of the lake and an opportunity for a brisk alpine dip before riding your legs back down the single-track.

There are several Class 2 13,000-foot peaks close to Columbine Lake, but given the loose nature of the rock, adding on any of these peaks would be hiking rather than running detours.

Given the mellow nature of the upper section of this running route, this makes a great option for alpine intervals in preparation for higher-elevation routes in the general vicinity: miles 1.6–2.8 involve only 250 feet of vertical gain.

After a fast final two miles, reach the ethereal blue lake hidden up this high valley. Photo by Tony Vazquez

COLUMBINE LAKE

MATTERHORN CREEK

26

Total Distance	6.7 miles (out-and-back)
Starting Elevation	10,385 feet
High Point Elevation	12,760 feet
Total Elevation Gain	2,465 feet
Difficulty	● Beginner
Round-trip Time	1.5–2 hours
Runability	95%
Nearest Town	Lake City

COMMENT: Rising from an ancient volcanic basin, Wetterhorn Peak and Uncompahgre Peak are two particularly unique-looking Colorado 14ers. The high-alpine meadows around them are rich with columbine, Indian paintbrush, pikas, and marmots too numerous to count. This run takes you on a tour of the basin to the south of the peaks.

GETTING THERE: From Lake City, head west on Second Street to the turn for the Alpine Scenic Loop Byway. Follow this west for 8.9 miles until you reach the right-hand fork for North Fork Henson Creek/FSR 870. From here, 8+ inches of clearance

Around 1.5 miles in, the Wetterhorn–Matterhorn ridgeline comes into view.

From the base of Wetterhorn, turn around for a quick and mellow descent, but first, take in the view of Uncompahgre Peak to the east.

and 4WD are essential. Navigate your vehicle another 2 miles to the lower Matter-horn Creek Trailhead at 10,385 feet. Mountain bikers can ride here, but the only available places to stash bikes are alongside trees.

THE ROUTE: Start up the road for the first 0.6 mile. This 4WD road section is a great warm-up for the single-track to come. Focus on your feet as you wind through mixed forest up to the trailhead. Reach it at 10,800 feet as the road fades into single-track and you pass the trailhead sign.

This part of the San Juans has particularly interesting geological quirks. This specific basin is remnant from volcanic activity; geologists have identified at least three distinct lava flows that formed the ridgelines in the basin. As the trees thin, notice how your northbound path contours the western slopes of a lower ridge on the southern rim of the basin. Descend and ascend several rolls in terrain as you cross four tributary streams.

At 2.4 miles and 11,990 feet, some gentle switchbacks and two more tributary stream crossings bring you into the broad, verdant floor of the high basin, with the Wetterhorn and Matterhorn massif and the monumental ramp of Uncompahgre rising into view to your north and east. Nicknamed "King of the San Juans," Uncompahgre is the highest mountain in the range and the sixth highest in Colorado at 14,321 feet. Its name is Ute for "red spring water," and it is one of the five 14ers in

Though not recommended as part of your run, the Class 3 scramble of Wetterhorn Peak is reached by this trail, and yields phenomenal views.

Colorado for which a native name is also the USGS recognized name. Wetterhorn and Matterhorn, meanwhile, are named for Swiss peaks they resemble, though they are respectively higher and lower than their physically distant namesakes.

A good turnaround point for this run is at 3.4 miles and 12,760 feet. While this easy path continues up Wetterhorn Peak, the Class 3 14er requires a helmet and intermediate routefinding skills on rock across gullies that are not runnable. It is not recommended to attempt running the mountain. Enjoy your easy jaunt on these alpine trails under the sundial wedge of the King of the San Juans before returning to Lake City.

MATTERHORN CREEK

HANDIES PEAK

27

Total Distance	8.2 miles (out-and-back)
Starting Elevation	10,420 feet
High Point Elevation	14,048 feet
Total Elevation Gain	3,650 feet
Difficulty	■ Intermediate
Round-trip Time	2.5–4 hours
Runability	85%
Nearest Town	Lake City
Add-on	American Basin Trail (loop)

COMMENT: One of the high points of the Hardrock 100 ultramarathon, Handies Peak offers a stunning viewpoint of surrounding lakes, rolling alpine meadows, and ragged ridges of nearby 13ers. The East Slopes trail crosses through meadow after meadow of wildflowers, including a palette of multicolored Indian paintbrush.

GETTING THERE: From Lake City, take CO Highway 149 south for 2.5 miles. Then turn west (right) onto CR 30 and drive 16.2 miles to the Silver Creek/Grizzly Gulch Trailhead. Do not turn left onto CR 35 toward Cataract Gulch after the Grizzly RT

In midsummer, the Indian paintbrush make a wonderful foreground.

Just above tree line, look at the gorgeous upper basin.

RV Park; continue west-northwest on CR 30. This road can vary in condition. A high-clearance 4WD vehicle can reach this trailhead easily. Lower-clearance vehicles can access this trailhead in most years, but at least 7 inches of clearance is necessary and drivers will want to be comfortable on rocky and narrow roads. This road is not recommended for mountain bikes, as it is popular among ATV 4-wheelers and can be very dusty.

THE ROUTE: Head west from the signed Grizzly Gulch Trailhead, and immediately cross a bridge over Lake Fork Creek. The trail parallels Grizzly Creek southwest up the valley; you are never far from water. Recent trail work has made this approach a runner's dream, with smooth log steps marking out much of the first mile as the trail ascends through old-growth coniferous forest.

After passing through several meadows between stands of boreal forest, which are signs of winter avalanche activity, you clear tree line around 1.8 miles into the broad east-facing basin. These alpine wildflower meadows give scope to the name Indian paintbrush, as midsummer excursions yield shades of pink, magenta, and maroon beyond counting, in addition to other species of flora, such as the classic

The summit views to the northeast show several of the nearby runs.

columbine and regal King's Crown. Also keep a sharp eye out for the endangered Uncompahgre fritillary butterflies, small orange pollinators with brown-and-black wing markings. In the winter, this basin holds a significant amount of snow, so most summers the wildflowers flourish along the rivulets that feed into Grizzly Creek.

At 2.4 miles and 12,360 feet, the trail starts to become steadily steeper, with more switchbacks, as it ascends toward the ridge that runs from Handies east to 13er Whitecross Mountain. Gain the ridge at 13,590 feet and get your first peek into the American Basin, the Class 1 route for the peak.

Handies Peak, at 14,048 feet, offers striking geologic views. Nearby peaks vary from dramatic to gently rolling. Close to the east-northeast are Redcloud Peak and Sunshine Peak, easily distinguishable by their respective red and yellow tinges. Due north, Uncompahgre Peak and Wetterhorn Peak thrust dramatically into the skyline.

From a relatively small summit, it is 4.1 miles back down Grizzly Gulch to the trailhead. If you prefer to make your run a longer loop, descend down the American Basin Trail to County Road 12 and then County Road 30. This offers a change of scenery and passes by the lovely cerulean Sloan Lake, headwater of Lake Fork Creek. The loop option adds another 7.3 miles for an 11.1-mile day.

HANDIES PEAK

COOPER LAKE

28

Total Distance	10 miles (out-and-back)
Starting Elevation	10,420 feet
High Point Elevation	12,800 feet
Total Elevation Gain	2,380 feet
Difficulty	■ Intermediate
Round-trip Time	2.5–3.5 hours
Runability	95%
Nearest Town	Lake City

COMMENT: Make an action-packed running-camping weekend at the Grizzly Gulch Trailhead by running this route the day before or after Handies Peak, which shares the trailhead. Cooper Lake is a hidden gem up the valley to the west of the Silver Creek valley. The good trail and the solitude make for an ideal trail run with a challenging finish.

GETTING THERE: From Lake City, take CO Highway 149 south for 2.5 miles. Then turn west (right) onto CR 30 and drive 16.2 miles to the Silver Creek/Grizzly Gulch Trailhead. Do not turn left onto CR 35 toward Cataract Gulch after the Grizzly RT RV Park; continue west-northwest on CR 30. This road can vary in condition. A high-clearance 4WD vehicle can reach this trailhead easily. Lower-clearance vehicles can access this trailhead in most years, but drivers will want to be comfortable

The mellow ascent through gorgeous alpine meadows

Cooper Lake and the upper sections of the Cooper Creek valley as seen from the summit of Gudy Peak due west of the lake.

on rocky and narrow roads, and at least 7 inches of clearance is necessary. This road is not recommended for mountain bikers, as it is popular among ATV 4-wheelers and thus can be very dusty.

THE ROUTE: Start out running west on CR 30 for the first 0.8 mile. Right before the Cooper Creek Trailhead, pass the informational sign for the historical Argentum mining camp site. Turn northeast (right) here to get onto the single-track. Weave through a small section of coniferous forest along switchbacks. The trail gradually

As you gain elevation, look back across the valley and catch a glimpse of Handies and Whitecross Peaks.

Cooper Lake offers lovely views but cannot itself be seen even from nearby 14ers.

gains elevation for the next 1.4 miles. Cross Cooper Creek at 11,208 feet. If early in the summer, you may be able to use a snowbridge for this crossing. Otherwise, look carefully for logs and stones to pick your way across the heavily mineralized water.

After the crossing, you only have 0.5 mile left within tree line as you move into untouched alpine meadows. Time your run early in the morning to enjoy the sunrise, as beams of light creep over the 13,000-foot ridgeline at the east end of the valley like Beatles lyrics. The trail runs closely alongside Cooper Creek for most of the next mile, so your feet may get damp in the sections closest to the water or while recrossing the creek if you are exploring the route in early summer.

At 3.5 miles and 11,600 feet, the trail starts to steadily gain elevation. As switch-backs begin, the trail turns west and the route gains another 1,200 vertical feet in the remaining 1.5 mile to the lake. At mile 4.5 (12,400 feet), you may want to switch to a power hike to follow the now-thin trail up steep, loose switchbacks for the final 0.5 mile. Running poles will come in handy here.

Breathe deeply and maintain a steady pace, knowing that in the final 0.1 mile, the grade relaxes and your goal—a hidden glacial lake—appears. Continue to the west side of Cooper Lake to be able to fully appreciate the sapphire color of the water and the backdrop of the ridgeline separating this valley from the Silver Creek valley.

COOPER LAKE

N
Cooper Creek
10200
10400
10000
10600
10900
11600
11800
12000
12200
12400
12600
11600
11400
12000
11800
10800
11000
10200
11600
11400
12000
12800
12600
11000
Peak 13520
12200
13000
12800
12400
13200
12800
12600
11800
Cooper Lake
Gudy Peak
0.2mi
0.3mi
0.4mi
13000
12200
Cooper Creek
12000
11800
12800
13200
13000
CT Peak
0.5mi
0.7mi
12400
12200
11400
11600
0.3mi
12600
12800
1.0mi
12400
12000
11800
0.6mi
11600
11200
10800
Lake Fork
CR 30
10800
Handies Peak Wilderness Study Area
11200
11400
11600
11800
12000
12400
12600
11400
11000
0.4mi
0.4mi
11200
11000
Silver Creek
11400
11800
South Fork
0.3mi
Trailhead
0.4mi
Whitecross Mountain
12400
12600
11000
11200
11600
11000
10600
12000
13000
13200
12400
MILES
0
0.5
1
1.5

REDCLOUD PEAK

29

Total Distance	9 miles (out-and-back)
Starting Elevation	10,420 feet
High Point Elevation	14,034 feet
Total Elevation Gain	3,700 feet
Difficulty	■ Intermediate
Round-trip Time	2.5–4 hours
Runability	75%
Nearest Town	Lake City
Add-on	Sunshine Peak (14,001 feet)

COMMENT: The high-alpine meadows surrounding Redcloud Peak are the heart of a conservation area designated for Uncompahgre fritillary butterflies. These wildflower meadows are especially gorgeous with the contrast of the rich red soil of the peak. This route has a delightful mix of single-track through forest, meadow, and across alpine talus.

Wetterhorn and Uncompahgre Peaks as seen from the shoulder of Redcloud Peak.

From Redcloud's summit, there are gorgeous views of the San Juans, particularly Wetterhorn and Uncompahgre to the north.

GETTING THERE: From Lake City, take CO Highway 149 south for 2.5 miles. Then turn west onto CR 30 and drive 16.2 miles to the Silver Creek/Grizzly Gulch Trailhead. Do not turn left onto CR 35 toward Cataract Gulch after the Grizzly RT RV Park; continue west-northwest on CR 30. This road can vary in condition. A high-clearance 4WD vehicle can reach this trailhead easily. Lower- clearance vehicles can access this trailhead in most years, but drivers will want to be comfortable on rocky and narrow roads, and at least 7 inches of clearance is necessary. This road is not recommended for mountain bikers, as it is popular among ATV 4-wheelers and thus can be very dusty.

THE ROUTE: Start northeast up the Silver Creek Trail and enter the trees quickly as you leave the clearing of the parking area and dispersed camping behind. Pace yourself as you warm up on these gentle switchbacks through mixed forest. The valley grows narrower as you ascend. Within 0.2 mile, you are closely paralleling Silver Creek as the single-track trail crosses sections of talus and alluvial fans accumulated from years of winter and spring avalanches.

At 2 miles and 11,700 feet, leave tree line behind for good as the 13,000-foot ridge connecting Redcloud to nearby peaks comes into full view. Redcloud itself remains hidden to your southeast, side ridges hiding the distinctive summit from

Indian paintbrush decorating the Silver Creek basin

view. This next stretch of trail is crowded with willows vying for the water of the mineral-rich, bluish-white Silver Creek. By mile 2.3, around 12,000 feet, the willows are more dwarfed by the altitude. The occasional glacial erratic boulder spots the meadow. Marmots use many of these boulders as burrow landmarks and basking platforms, so take care not to disturb them should you pause for a break. The trail begins turning east and then southward, which brings the saddle between Redcloud and nearby, unnamed Centennial peaks into view. The route grows steep and your upper switchbacks begin at 3.3 miles and 12,600 feet.

Now fully on talus single-track, 1.2 miles and 1,400 feet remain to the summit. Settle into a power hike. Take a right (west) at the saddle at 3.6 miles to stay on more established trail toward your peak. The false summit is now within view as the upper stretches of the trail become visible along the ridge crest. Move steadily southwest and step onto the flat red summit at 14,034 feet.

If you're up for an extra challenge, consider adding Sunshine Peak. The lowest Colorado 14er, at 14,001 feet, Sunshine's bright yellow summit provides a striking contrast to Redcloud. Do not add this peak unless the skies and forecast are clear, as the path is completely exposed, never dipping below 13,500, and there are no safe alternative bailouts. Adding Sunshine is an extra 3.2 miles and 1,100 feet vertical round-trip. If you start your run intending to do both peaks, be sure to bring at least an additional half liter of water and extra calories.

REDCLOUD PEAK

THE WINDOW

30

Total Distance	24.8 miles (out-and-back)
Starting Elevation	9,350 feet
High Point Elevation	13,057 feet
Total Elevation Gain	4,900 feet
Difficulty	◆◆ Most Difficult
Round-trip Time	6–8.5 hours
Runability	80%
Nearest Towns	Creede/Lake City

COMMENT: This endurance gem takes you deep into the Weminuche Wilderness. The terrain shifts from north-facing forested single-track to aspen-stand switchbacks to temperate wetland to high glacially carved basins. Be prepared to get deep enough into the backcountry that it feels like time travel.

GETTING THERE: Turn south off of CO Highway 149 onto CR 520. Heading west from Creede, this is a left at 20 miles; heading southeast from Lake City, it is a right at

A runner looks west toward The Window and Rio Grande Pyramid.

Left: At 5.4 miles, continue straight south. **Right:** The next fork comes at 6.4 miles. Take a slight right and start turning westward.

30.4 miles. Follow the dirt road for 11.2 miles. Vehicles with 4WD and at least 5 inches of clearance are recommended. Take a left at Thirty Mile Campground and park in the overflow lot; the signed trailhead is 0.1 mile due south past some campsites.

THE ROUTE: From the trailhead, turn right (west). The initial miles of trail contour along the southern side of Rio Grande Reservoir before plunging southward into deeper wilderness. As this is a big run in a remote area, I suggest pausing at the trail register about 100 feet past the trailhead to sign your name and destination. The first 2 miles provide an excellent warm-up on rolling trail through mixed forest. Settle into a comfortable and sustainable jog and enjoy the expansive view of the reservoir on your right.

At 9,830 feet, the trail begins contouring southward. A mere 0.3 mile later, cross Weminuche Creek via a log bridge and consider switching to a power hike. You'll gain 310 feet in the next 0.4 mile. Manage your pace carefully in this section as you work your way up steady switchbacks. The trail will carry you through aspen groves as well as mixed forest. At 10,290 feet and 2.8 miles, the terrain becomes gentler and the forest more open. Enjoy the next few miles of rolling terrain, excellent for a casual jogging pace.

Watch the trail very carefully starting at mile 5. The first fork you come to, marked by a cairn at mile 5.5, is not the recommended one. Wait until mile 6.5, when you are moving along open terrain along the edge of the broad temperate wetland. Your elevation will be around 10,600 feet. A faint trail fork is marked by a

Left: From the summit of Window Peak, Centennial's Rio Grande Pyramid looms one mile to the north. **Right:** At 12.7 miles and 1 mile into your descent, take in The Window and Rio Grande Pyramid from a small tarn along the trail.

weathered post. Take the narrower trail to the right and turn west toward the forest and the massif. If running in late July to mid-August, expect the next several miles of trail to be lush with wild strawberries and some wild raspberries. While sections of this stretch are extremely runnable, the urge to forage may slow you down.

The next section of switchbacks begins at mile 7.9, after you pass through the grassy open wash and catch a glimpse of your destination. Gain 1,240 feet over the next 2 miles as you navigate up this ridge through coniferous forest and then along the southern edge of a talus field. Patience pays; at the top of this section, one last gradual stretch and one more ascent remain. The tributary creek parallel to the trail between miles 9 and 10 is your best option for refilling water should you need to do so.

Reach the plateau at 9.9 miles. Now at 12,130 feet and the upper terminus of tree line, you are in the shadow of the Centennial peak Rio Grande Pyramid, The Window, and Window Peak. Take in the views of the weathered terrain as you follow the thin trail southward. After passing below the eastern sides of The Window and Window Peak, reach the top of a pass at 11.9 miles and 12,610 feet.

Turn right (north) onto a faint trail to complete the final 0.5 mile to the top of Window Peak. Enjoy striking views of the Grenadiers to the west, The Window and Rio Grande Pyramid to the north, and the rolling, glacially shaped basins to your south and east. After a revitalizing snack, retrace your steps for the 12.4-mile trip back to the trailhead.

THE WINDOW

Trailhead
Rio Grande Reservoir
Simpson Mountain
Peak 12045
Peak 12334
Peak 13261
Peak 13278
Peak 12724
Rio Grande Pyramid
Window Peak
Peak 13017
Peak 12881
Peak 12822
Ute Benchmark
CDT
5.0mi
6.3mi
3.7mi
2.8mi
4.1mi
1.4mi
0.9mi
0.5mi
1.6mi
0.6mi
0.4mi
2.5mi
6.0mi
3.1mi
N
MILES
0
1
2
3
4
5
6
7
8

SANGRE DE CRISTO RANGE

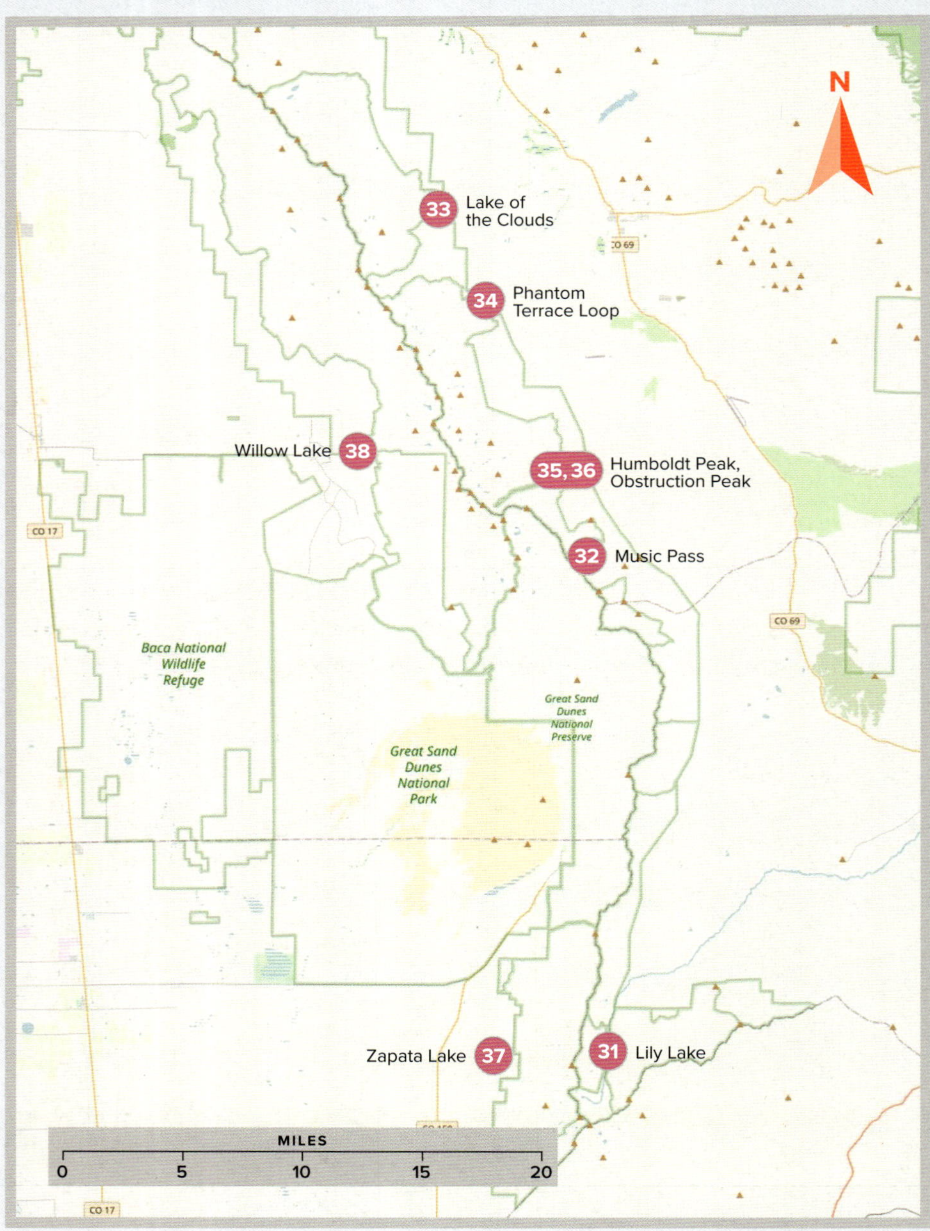

COLORADO ALPINE TRAIL RUNS

LILY LAKE

31

Total Distance	6.8 miles (out-and-back)
Starting Elevation	10,615 feet
High Point Elevation	12,310 feet
Total Elevation Gain	1,700 feet
Difficulty	● Beginner
Round-trip Time	1.25–2 hours
Runability	90%
Nearest Town	Gardner

COMMENT: Lily Lake is tucked beneath the northern ridgeline of 14,042-foot peak Ellingwood Point. It offers dramatic views of Mount Lindsey and Huerfano Peak to the east and the sharp spine of the Sangre de Cristos to the immediate west.

GETTING THERE: From Gardner, drive west on CO Highway 69 for 0.5 mile. Turn left (south) onto Mosca Pass Road (CR 550). Follow for 11.8 miles, then take a left onto Forest Road 580. Continue another 7.7 miles, passing the entrances for Singing

Just after the trailhead, take in the early morning light on Mount Lindsey to the south.
Photo by Robin Lindsay

For unique views of 14er Ellingwood Point, continue a quarter mile north of the lake. Photo by Robin Lindsay

River Ranch and Aspen River Ranch. The last mile to the parking for the Lily Lake and Huerfano trailheads requires at least 8 inches of clearance and 4WD.

THE ROUTE: Start on the Upper Huerfano/Lily Lake Trailhead with multiple 13ers and 14ers looming to your south. This first mile of trail along Huerfano River is low and damp. Especially in June and July, this valley-floor section of trail can resemble wetland rather than neatly separated trail and creek, so be prepared for wet feet on this short jaunt. At the signed trail fork, turn right (southwest) onto the Lily Lake Trail. From this point, start gaining elevation.

The next 1.8 miles are gradual, and you'll gain another 800 feet in the intermittent forest and meadows. You'll be able to maintain a quick pace on the well-maintained trail. This is a more solitary part of the Sangre de Cristos; relish the riverside miles. Once you've reached the 2.8-mile point at 11,560 feet, take a sharp right turn to the northwest to start heading up switchbacks that will carry you above tree line.

Cross the upper sections of the Huerfano River three times over the next 0.6 mile. Given the 750-foot vertical gain, you may want to settle into a power hike. At 12,300 feet, reach this gem of a lake and take in the gorgeous surrounding ridgelines. It is possible to add 0.25 mile talus-hopping around the main lake and the upper lake before hitting your descent.

LILY LAKE

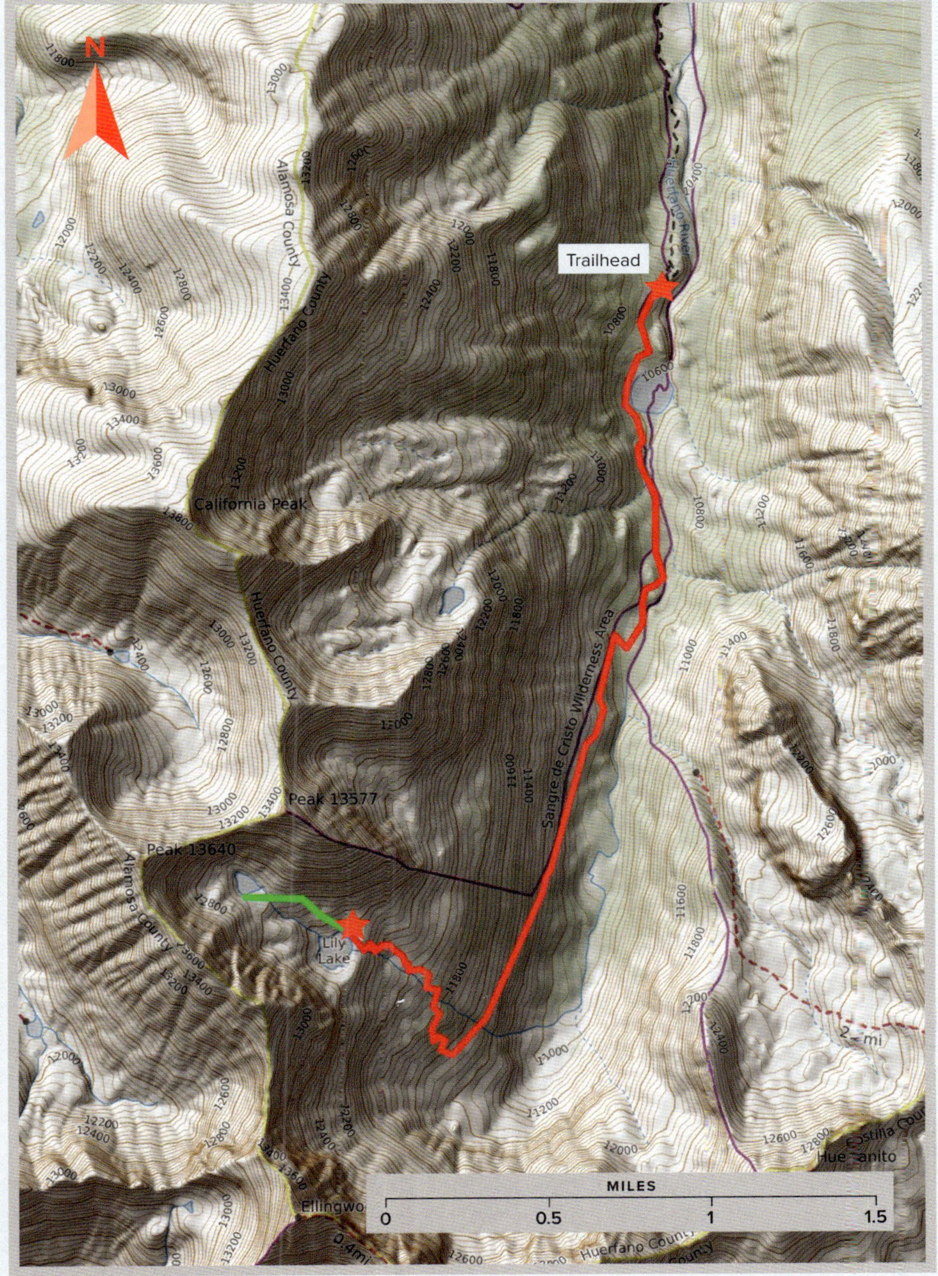

Lily Lake

MUSIC PASS

32

Total Distance	7.2 miles (out-and-back)
Starting Elevation	9,310 feet
High Point Elevation	11,400 feet
Total Elevation Gain	2,090 feet
Difficulty	● Beginner
Round-trip Time	1.5–2 hours
Runability	80%
Nearest Town	Westcliffe
Add-ons	Lower Sand Creek Lake (■ Intermediate), Marble Mountain A (13,266 feet, ◆ Difficult)

COMMENT: Music Pass is a good acclimation run when arriving in the Sangre de Cristos. It can also be the access point for some delightful skyrunning, should you choose to ascend Marble Mountain A during your excursion. Alternately, for a lake run, you can descend to Lower Sand Creek Lake.

Looking back down the southern ridgeline between Music Pass and Marble Mountain A. This is idyllic off-trail skyrunning.

A broad point of the ridge looking northwest to the summit of Marble Mountain A

GETTING THERE: From Westcliffe, head 4.5 miles south on US Highway 69, then turn right (west) onto Colfax Lane and continue 5.6 miles. Turn left (south) onto South Colony Road for 0.7 mile until you turn onto FSR 119. The Music Pass Trailhead is 4.5 miles from this turn. If you have a lower-clearance vehicle, consider parking at Grape Creek Trailhead (9,310 feet), which will add 4 miles and 1,400 feet vertical gain to your round-trip excursion. High-clearance 4WD vehicles can continue to Music Pass Trailhead.

THE ROUTE: If starting your run at Grape Creek Trailhead, follow the road 2.4 miles to the upper Music Pass Trailhead. As this road can get quite dusty, consider carrying extra water and a face covering. Gain 1,300 feet over this stretch. As the forest around you transitions from aspen stands to boreal, reach the Music Pass Trailhead.

This broad trail meanders upward and southwest from the upper trailhead, snaking through forest as nearby summits occasionally peek through the trees. The further you gain toward Music Pass, the more likely you are to feel that you have been transported into the central Alps. From the upper trailhead, it is a mere 740 vertical feet across 1.2 miles to the top of the pass. Enjoy this run to tree line and the views of the Music valley. This context may feel especially strong at the top of

A view of the Sand Creek Basin and lakes, an alternate add-on for the route

the pass. From the broad saddle, the Sand Creek Lakes sparkle beneath dramatic, spiky ridgelines.

From the top of Music Pass, there are two options to extend your run. If you want to stay below 11,500 feet, continue heading west for 1.1 miles to Lower Sand Creek Lake. This is a gently rolling run and a nice warm-up for the Sangre de Cristos. From Lower Sand Creek Lake, the view of Music Mountain is even more immediate overhead. This add-on makes for a total of 9.4 miles and 3,175 feet of vertical gain round-trip.

The second option from the top of the pass packs on 1,840 feet of vertical gain in 2.5 miles and takes you to the top of Marble Mountain A at 13,266 feet. This is true adventure running. For this add-on, leave the trail at the top of Music Pass and head northwest in a steady power hike, gaining 1,100 feet over 0.75 mile. By the time you reach the top of the ridge, you are past tree line and the horizon opens up.

From here, the slope grade relaxes and the views become incredible. Though the next 1.6 miles gain only 800 feet, the ridgeline offers dramatic views in complement to sturdy foot placements. The vantage point from this ridgeline shows the steep exposure from the top of Music Mountain down to Lower Sand Creek Lake to the west, while the 14,000-foot Humboldt and the Crestones cluster to your northwest. Enjoy the solitude on this low summit before turning and heading southeast down the ridgeline. This ridge run brings your route total to 12.3 miles and 5,000 vertical feet.

MUSIC PASS

Lower Trailhead
Upper Trailhead
Loco Hill
Middle Knob
Grape Creek
San Isabel National Forest
County 119
119
Colfax
CR 119
FS 119
FS 119
Rainbow 1336
Beck Mountain
Music Pass Creek
Hudson Creek
Snowslide Mountain
Custer County
Saguache County
Sangre de Cristo Wilderness Area
Custer County
Saguache County
Marble Mountain
1.9mi.
1.3mi.
Lower Sand Creek Lake
Upper Sand Creek Lake
Music Mountain
Wadlee Peak 13261
Tijeras Peak 13604
Peak 13401
MILES
0
1
2
3
4
N

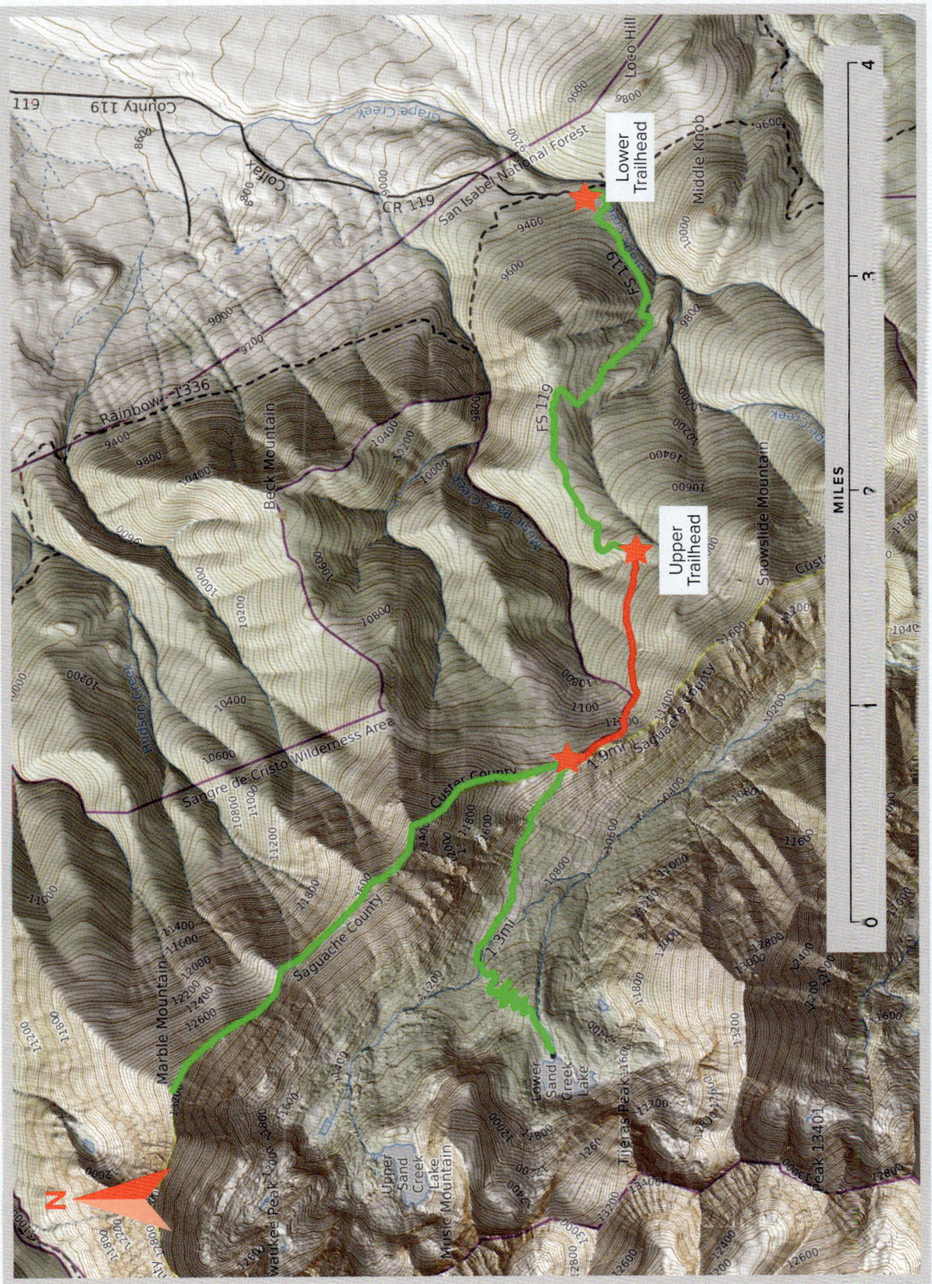

LAKE OF THE CLOUDS

33

Total Distance	10.2 miles (out-and-back)
Starting Elevation	9,480 feet
High Point Elevation	11,665 feet
Total Elevation Gain	2,190 feet
Difficulty	■ Intermediate
Round-trip Time	2–3.5 hours
Runability	85%
Nearest Town	Westcliffe

COMMENT: This lake run meanders through the woods alongside Swift Creek. The three Lakes of the Clouds top out at tree line around 11,600 feet. This route is a great acclimation run before some of the higher and more exposed routes in the Sangre de Cristos. This run is best in the early morning or evening before sunset to avoid the heat. Like most non-14er trails in the eastern Sangre de Cristos, you do not need to worry about heavy foot traffic here. While you will encounter some hikers and fishermen, expect relative solitude.

The view southwest toward Peak of the Clouds from the uppermost lake

Looking back down-trail at the top of your descent

GETTING THERE: From Westcliffe, turn west off of US Highway 69 onto CR 160 (Hermit Road) and follow for 5.9 miles. Continue as it turns into Sampson Ridge Road for 1.6 miles. It then becomes North Taylor Road and turns to dirt for 0.9 mile to the Gibson Creek Trailhead. Park in the small dirt parking lot.

THE ROUTE: From the parking lot, head north toward the Rainbow Trail and follow it for 0.6 mile. Be sure not to gain more than 150 feet; this thin trail can be easy to lose if not paying close attention. Reach the Swift Creek Trail #1351 and turn left (west). Follow this broad sandy trail for 2.5 miles, gaining 1,350 vertical feet through mixed forest. Though small sections are steep, much of this stretch is highly runnable.

Reach the junction with the Lakes of the Clouds Trail #1349 and turn left. Here, the trail becomes steeper as the forest thins out. After 1.5 miles, reach the first lake. To reach tree line, follow the trail another 0.7 mile. This affords a great view of the lakes from above and a great reflection of any clouds in the water. Spread Eagle Peak and Peak of the Clouds loom above you to the south with classic Sangre prominence.

These lakes make a great spot to pause for a snack before turning and following the trail back down to the Gibson Creek Trailhead. Enjoy stretching your legs and see how quickly you can wend your way through the trees back to the car.

Should you choose to explore the creek that runs between the lakes, you can find this peekaboo view of Peak of the Clouds.

LAKE OF THE CLOUDS

PHANTOM TERRACE LOOP

34

Total Distance	12.6 miles (loop)
Starting Elevation	8,920 feet
High Point Elevation	12,850 feet
Total Elevation Gain	4,400 feet
Difficulty	◆ Difficult
Round-trip Time	4–6 hours
Runability	85%
Nearest Town	Westcliffe
Add-on	Comanche Peak (13,277 feet) and Spring Mountain (13,244 feet)

COMMENT: This nearly half-marathon loop offers excellent views of the jagged and narrow Sangre de Cristo Range as well as the broad valleys to the east and west. Should you be in the mood for some classic ridgy skyrunning, you can safely do a variation to include a few 13,000-foot summits and about 1,500 feet extra vertical gain.

The view south toward the Crestones from the ridgeline variation

GETTING THERE: From Westcliffe, follow CO Highway 69 southwest for 3.3 miles. Turn west (right) onto CR 140 (Schoolfield Road) and follow it for 6.5 miles. Take a right onto CR 148 and head up a short section of dirt switchbacks to the cement parking area for both the Venable and Comanche trailheads.

THE ROUTE: One of the most unique trails on the east side of the Sangre de Cristos, this run offers both gorgeous and mellow single-track as well as exposure more comparable to summit running routes. This route has lakes and creeks that can be used for water refills during the first and last quarters, so it is recommended to bring a form of water treatment or filter.

The Venable and Comanche trailheads sit on either side of a level, reasonably protected parking lot, and they provide convenient access to these neighboring valleys as well as the Rainbow Trail. To do this loop clockwise, start up the Comanche Trail on the south side of the parking area. Popular with backpackers, the trail offers leisurely switchbacks through mixed aspen and coniferous forest before crossing over a shoulder of ridge at 3.75 miles and turning west up the Comanche valley. The loop can also be run counterclockwise; if you choose to do so, follow these directions in reverse.

The trail traverses along south-facing slopes and across scree fields and avalanche aprons. Comanche Peak looms at the west side of the valley and turning to look back offers glimpses of the broad Wet Mountain Valley to the east, with Comanche Lake glittering below. Your path begins to sneak upward through waist-high willows at mile 5.2 and gains the narrow saddle below Comanche Peak at mile 6.3.

From this saddle, turn right (north) for 1 mile. There is no sign, but this is the direction of the only maintained trail. From here, expect little vertical gain, but an ethereal view upon crossing the next saddle. The Phantom Terrace traverses below Venable Peak through steep maroon and eggshell cliffs. For those averse to heights, fear not: the trail is well-established and level. The terrace is short, only 0.6 mile. Shortly after, you can visit Venable Lake at 12,010 feet (8.25 miles) before letting your legs and gravity carry you back down to tree line and through the 4.4 miles of forest back to the trailhead.

VARIATION: If you prefer to add about 1,500 feet of vertical gain and some ridge running to your day, you can add on Comanche Peak and Spring Mountain For this option, head south (hard left) from the Comanche saddle (mentioned above), a 510-foot, 0.4-mile jaunt on faint trail. The summit of Comanche Peak offers stunning views south to the Crestones and impressive exposure over the Comanche valley.

Once you return to the saddle northbound, stay close to the ridgeline, gaining 530 feet over the next 0.6 mile to the summit of Spring Mountain. Here, make sure to look south again for sweeping views of Sangre ridges and the Crestone cluster of Centennial peaks 6 miles to your south. From the summit of Spring Mountain, turn feet northward again and follow the ridge another 0.5 mile to the Venable saddle to rejoin the trail just in time to run across the Phantom Terrace.

The striking Phantom Terrace. It's all downhill from here.

PHANTOM TERRACE LOOP

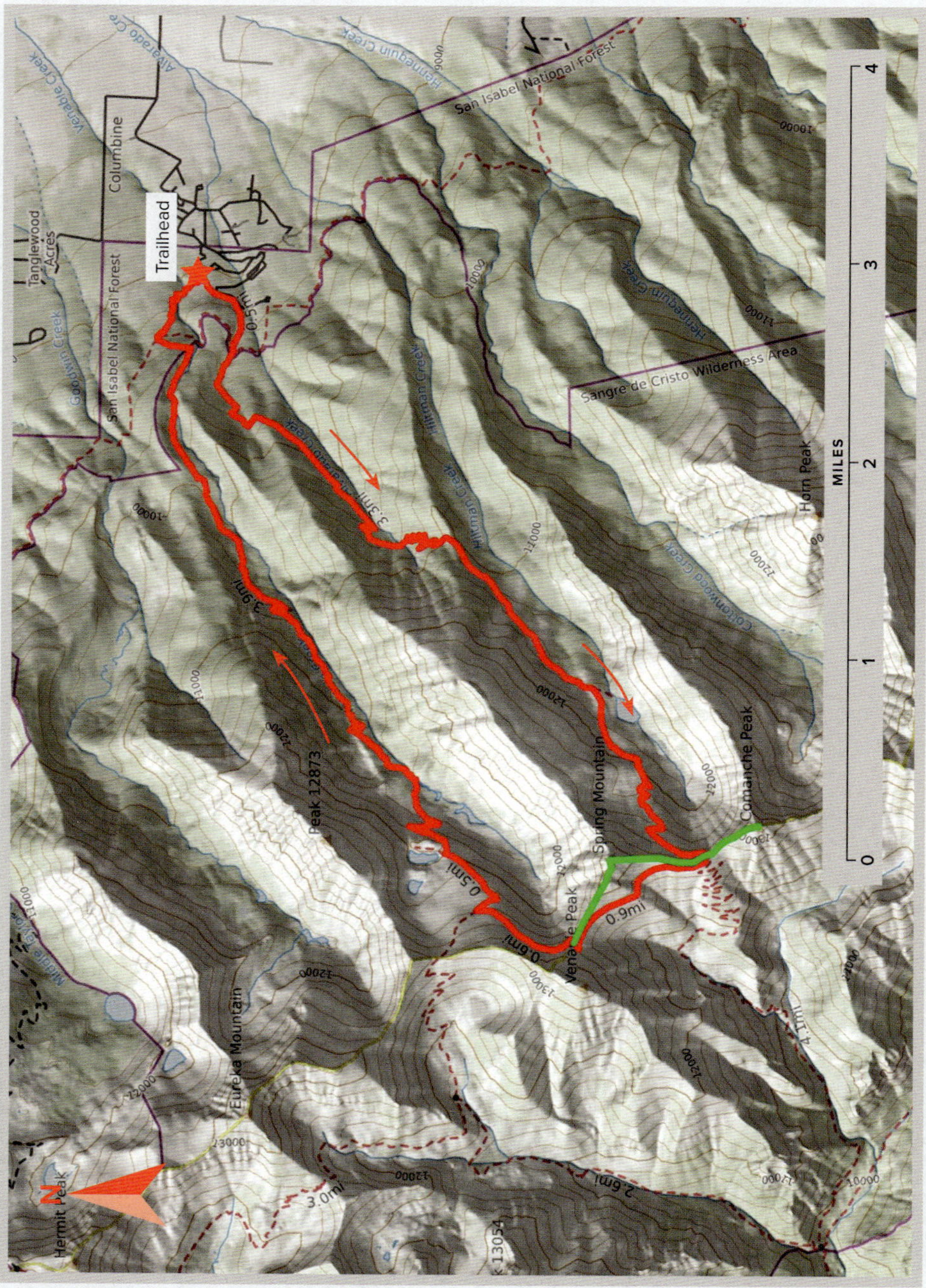

HUMBOLDT PEAK

35

Total Distance	9.8 miles (out-and-back)
Starting Elevation	9,950 feet
High Point Elevation	14,064 feet
Total Elevation Gain	4,200 feet
Difficulty	◆ Difficult
Round-trip Time	2.5–3.5 hours
Runability	70%
Nearest Town	Westcliffe

COMMENT: Humboldt Peak is the friendliest of the cluster of 14,000-foot peaks known as the Crestone Group. Its relatively gentle trail offers excitement via proximity to a precipitous drop on the northern side of the ridge, and the views of the menacing neighbor peaks are nothing short of spectacular.

GETTING THERE: From Westcliffe, drive 4.5 miles south on CO Highway 69. Turn right (south) onto Colfax Lane and follow 5.5 miles. Then take a right (west) onto dirt South Colony Road for 1.3 miles until you reach the lower parking near a cattle guard. Low-clearance and 2WD vehicles will need to park here, adding 2.7 miles of approach up the South Colony Road (FSR 120) and 1,150 additional vertical feet. High-clearance (10+ inches) 4WD vehicles can negotiate the additional miles to the upper South Colony Lakes parking lot. Experience on rough roads is very helpful.

THE ROUTE: The initial 2.5 miles from the upper parking lot ascend on a closed segment of road and are thus ideal for warming up your legs. From 2.5 to 3.8 miles, it is important to watch closely for trail signs as the forest and willows close to South Colony Lakes are dense. Make sure to keep right (on the South Colony Trail) at all signed trail forks to head toward Humboldt's West Ridge Trail rather than the precarious Broken Hand Pass on the opposite side of the basin. The final right turn you take below tree line occurs at 3.75 miles and 12,115 feet, as you reach the uppermost lake.

Once on the Humboldt trail, you'll quickly leave the lakes and tree line behind. It is only 0.3 mile from your right turn to the Humboldt saddle, yet 700 vertical feet. You may prefer to power hike this section; a benefit of so doing is more time to take pictures of the dramatic nearby ridgelines while you ascend. Once you've reached the saddle, turn right again to stay on the well-established trail and head eastward toward the summit. Just 0.8 mile and 750 feet of ascent remain.

Looking up the west ridge from just west of the saddle with Obstruction Peak

COLORADO ALPINE TRAIL RUNS

The view of the Crestones and Bear's Playground from the summit

This upper section of trail is heavy with talus; make note of the best footing to prepare for your descent while you continue to push upward. Power hiking remains a reliable pacing option to avoid overexertion. Watch closely for turns and cairns as the trail becomes more subtle in the final 0.3 mile to the summit. Finally reach the broad, flat 14,064-foot high point, marked by several curved rock wind shelters. Catch your breath and admire the forbidding Crestones to the west before starting your careful, light-footed descent back down the ridge.

HUMBOLDT PEAK

OBSTRUCTION PEAK

36

Total Distance	12.8 miles (out-and-back)
Starting Elevation	9,950 feet
High Point Elevation	13,799 feet
Total Elevation Gain	4,700 feet
Difficulty	◆◆ Most Difficult
Round-trip Time	3–5 hours
Runability	70%
Nearest Town	Westcliffe

COMMENT: Some of the best alpine views to be found are not from the highest summits, but rather from other high points nearby. Obstruction Peak, situated in between five 14,000-foot peaks, is one of these. This partially off-trail route offers excellent ridge running and sweeping perspectives of the Sangre de Cristo Range.

Heading west, Crestone Needle and Peak dominate your southern horizon from Bear's Playground.

GETTING THERE: From Westcliffe, drive 4.5 miles south on CO Highway 69. Turn right (south) onto Colfax Lane (CR 119) and follow it for 5.5 miles. Then take a right onto dirt South Colony Road for 1.3 miles until you reach the lower parking near a cattle guard. Low-clearance and 2WD vehicles will need to park here, adding 2.7 miles of approach up the South Colony Road (FSR 120) and 1,150 additional vertical feet. High-clearance (10+ inches) 4WD vehicles can negotiate the additional miles to the upper parking lot. Experience on rough roads is very helpful. Although mountain bikers can ascend this road, it is not recommended given the 4-wheeling traffic and rougher rocky sections.

THE ROUTE: As with neighboring Humboldt Peak, the first 2.5 miles up the road from the upper trailhead are best used as a warm-up. The easy terrain through the trees passes quickly. Upon reaching the single-track near South Colony Lakes, stay right at the forks, following signs for Humboldt.

When you switch to a power hike as you leave tree line to head toward the Humboldt saddle, relish this maintained trail. It's a steep 0.3 mile to the Humboldt saddle at 12,850 feet, where you will turn west, away from the clear trail onto a thin, faint community path that follows close to this ridge crest.

Continue westward for 0.6 mile as you head toward the broad, high meadow known as Bear's Playground. While there are good, obvious foot placements along this stretch of ridge, it is narrow and this is your first sign of significant exposure on either side. Reach Bear's Playground at 5.8 miles and 13,200 feet. This gentle slope provides a beautiful foreground to the dramatic folded ridges of Crestone Needle and Peak to the southwest. Those steep peaks loom with startling immediacy over this mellow terrain despite sitting 0.6 mile away to the south. Turn roughly northward for steeper ascent toward your summit.

It is important to stay close to the ridge crest, keeping Bear's Playground to your left (south) to ensure you stay on route. Pick your way up the meadow for 0.2 mile, gaining 350 feet. Here, at 13,550 feet, the ridge grows narrower and steeper. Turn left (west) again to stay on the best footing. Your summit is only 0.1 mile and 250 feet away. Keep a steady pace until you top out at 6.4 miles and 13,799 feet. Pause for at least a few minutes to take in the drama of your surroundings.

The truest reward of off-trail alpine running is the descent. Brace yourself for the childlike exhilaration of racing downward through this alpine meadow, building steady momentum back to the Humboldt saddle, where you can accelerate down the switchbacks. You might even choose to take the 0.1-mile detour to dip into the nearest lake before closing the final miles back to the car.

From the top of Obstruction Peak, look eastward back at your return route.

OBSTRUCTION PEAK

ZAPATA LAKE

37

Total Distance	9.6 miles (out-and-back)
Starting Elevation	9,100 feet
High Point Elevation	11,930 feet
Total Elevation Gain	3,300 feet
Difficulty	■ Intermediate
Round-trip Time	3–4 hours
Runability	75%
Nearest Town	Mosca

COMMENT: This picturesque lake tucked far up Zapata Canyon is a serene hideaway from the popular Zapata Falls and nearby Great Sand Dunes. For this route, it is highly recommended that you run during full daylight and with a partner as mountain lions are active in the area.

Less than a mile in, the Great Sand Dunes and the Crestones peek through the trees to the north.

Zapata Lake

GETTING THERE: From CO Highway 150, turn east onto the Zapata Falls Road and follow it for 3.5 miles. You'll want 4WD and at least 5–6 inches of clearance, as stretches of the road are steep and rocky. Park at the Zapata Falls day trailhead rather than in the campground just south of the day lot.

THE ROUTE: Zapata Falls is a famous easy hike, the early stages of a gorge at a point where the creek is steadily gnawing through rock. It is a small, cool oasis hidden on the eastern margin of the dry San Luis Valley. Few tourists venture beyond the falls, which are less than 0.5 mile from the trailhead, and consequently miss the delights that wait beyond.

Make your way along the sandy trail as it switchbacks generally southeast. The first 0.5 mile ascends up a gentle sloping meadow toward the mouth of the Zapata Valley from which the falls pour. Pass the signed turnoff point for Zapata Falls at this half-mile mark, taking the right-hand turn to continue up sandy single-track. As the valley grows narrower, the slopes become steeper, particularly after the first creek crossing, which you'll cross via a fallen log.

These coming switchbacks gain steeply, taking you above 10,000 feet on narrow trail that passes below steep, chalky cliffs. Between miles 2.4 and 3, step over three small tributary streams in quick succession. Continue meandering up the valley, along talus fields and through patches of wild raspberries and flowers.

Left: One of the several creek crossings in the Zapata valley. Rocks can be damp and slick early in the morning, so mind your step! **Right:** At 4.3 miles, exit tree line. Zapata Lake is straight ahead.

Ellingwood Point as viewed from Zapata Lake

Reach the final significant stream crossing at mile 3.8 and 11,435 feet. Only 1.1 miles remain to the lake, in which you'll ascend through the last lingering stands of conifers and above tree line as the trail levels. The final 0.3 mile is nearly due south and rich with alpine flora. What snow falls in the winter and spring is protected by the north-facing valley and its steep walls, holding water to meter out gradually over the hot summer.

Relish a few moments at the lake; refill and treat your water if needed. Admire the looming summits of the 13,580-foot Twin Peaks to the west and 14,042-foot Ellingwood Point to the southeast. Then turn and keep high feet for a refreshing jaunt back down the valley.

ZAPATA LAKE

COLORADO ALPINE TRAIL RUNS

WILLOW LAKE

38

Total Distance	9.6 miles (out-and-back)
Starting Elevation	8,850 feet
High Point Elevation	11,765 feet
Total Elevation Gain	3,500 feet
Difficulty	■ Intermediate
Round-trip Time	2–3 hours
Runability	85%
Nearest Town	Crestone

COMMENT: A highly popular southern Colorado backpacking destination, Willow Lake is also a very pleasant run. It features a long, steady ascent on great trail and a fast, playful descent with plenty of fun corners for acceleration.

Willow Lake basin as seen from the north, with 14ers Humboldt Peak, Crestone Needle and Peak, Kit Carson Peak, and Challenger Point visible beyond the lake. The Blanca subrange looms on the horizon.

GETTING THERE: From CO Highway 17 in Moffat, turn east onto CR T toward Crestone. Follow 11.5 miles through town. Take a left on Alder Street and then a right onto Galena Street. After passing the grocery store, continue as the road turns to dirt and becomes Forest Service Road 949. From here, 7+ inches of clearance and 4WD are helpful. Follow 2 miles to the Willow Lake Trailhead. Because this is a very popular trail, starting very early in the morning or waiting until afternoon can be helpful to ensure you find a parking space.

THE ROUTE: Almost immediately after the trailhead, turn right (south) and cross South Crestone Creek. Follow the mellow, sandy switchbacks through high grasses and widely spaced trees for 1.1 miles. The flora here at the western foot of the Sangre de Cristos is a captivating mix of arid, resilient plant life as well as potent wild herbs such as the sunny-yellow arnica and purple wild aster along the trail.

At 1.3 miles, the trail carries you up and over a ridge (10,020 feet) to start contouring up the south-facing slopes running east toward the upper Willow Valley. The valley floor on your right is a lush, semi-annual wetland, the remnants of a lake long since filled in by the steady hand of time. Mile 2.2 heads back into steady switchbacks that offer peekaboo glimpses of the seeming headwall between the lower and upper valley. In midsummer you'll find wild raspberries galore, which thrive in the sandy, sun-drenched terrain. Mind your pace as you progress upward; while the grade of the trail is manageable, you still have many switchbacks to go.

Left: After 2.2 miles of manicured trail, things get spicier as you traverse and switchback rockier, talusy terrain. **Right:** Just above tree line, look west across Willow Lake before starting your descent.

The view from the Mount Adams basin down toward Willow Lake

Starting at 3.1 miles, the trail crosses several tributary segments of Willow Creek in a bare, cliffy area. This is your transition to more rugged terrain. Prepare to gain 400 feet over the next 0.4 mile on steeper, rockier trail, including making your way up six or seven switchbacks across a broad talus field. Once at the top of this talus at 11,240 feet, the terrain shifts significantly again. Watch your footing as the trail meanders eastward through damp, water-rich forest. It isn't visible itself, but the signs you are approaching Willow Lake grow ever clearer. The trail winds through dispersed campsites in addition to marshy depressions.

Reach the western edge of the lake at 4.3 miles and 11,570 feet, still below tree line. Continue for 0.5 mile more along the talus and willow-rimmed north edge of the lake to the broad rocky inflow on the eastern side of the lake. This gives you an open perspective from the top of Willow Falls, just above tree line. Although the trail continues to ascend, this is the recommended turnaround spot as the ascent heads up Challenger Point on loose rock and deteriorating trail. So rather than tacking on risky power hiking, turn around and push yourself on the descent.

WILLOW LAKE

Horn Lakes
Willow Creek Lakes
Peak 13517
Peak 13560
Mount Adams
Crestone Lake
Peak 13153
Peak 13546
South Crestone Lake
Crestone Peak
Challenge Point
Mt Carson Mountain
The Prow
Kitty Kat Carson
Kit Carson Mountain
Sangre de Cristo Wilderness Area
Willow Creek
Trailhead
FS 949 Rio Grande
South Crestone Creek
Panorama
Arrowhead
Hilltop
Darrell
Peaceful
Brookview
East Brook
Moonlight
Hillside
Broadview
MILES
0.8mi
1.3mi
0.3mi
0.7mi
1.3mi
0.2mi
0.3mi
1.2mi
1.3mi
1.0mi
0.2mi
1.9mi
N

SAWATCH RANGE

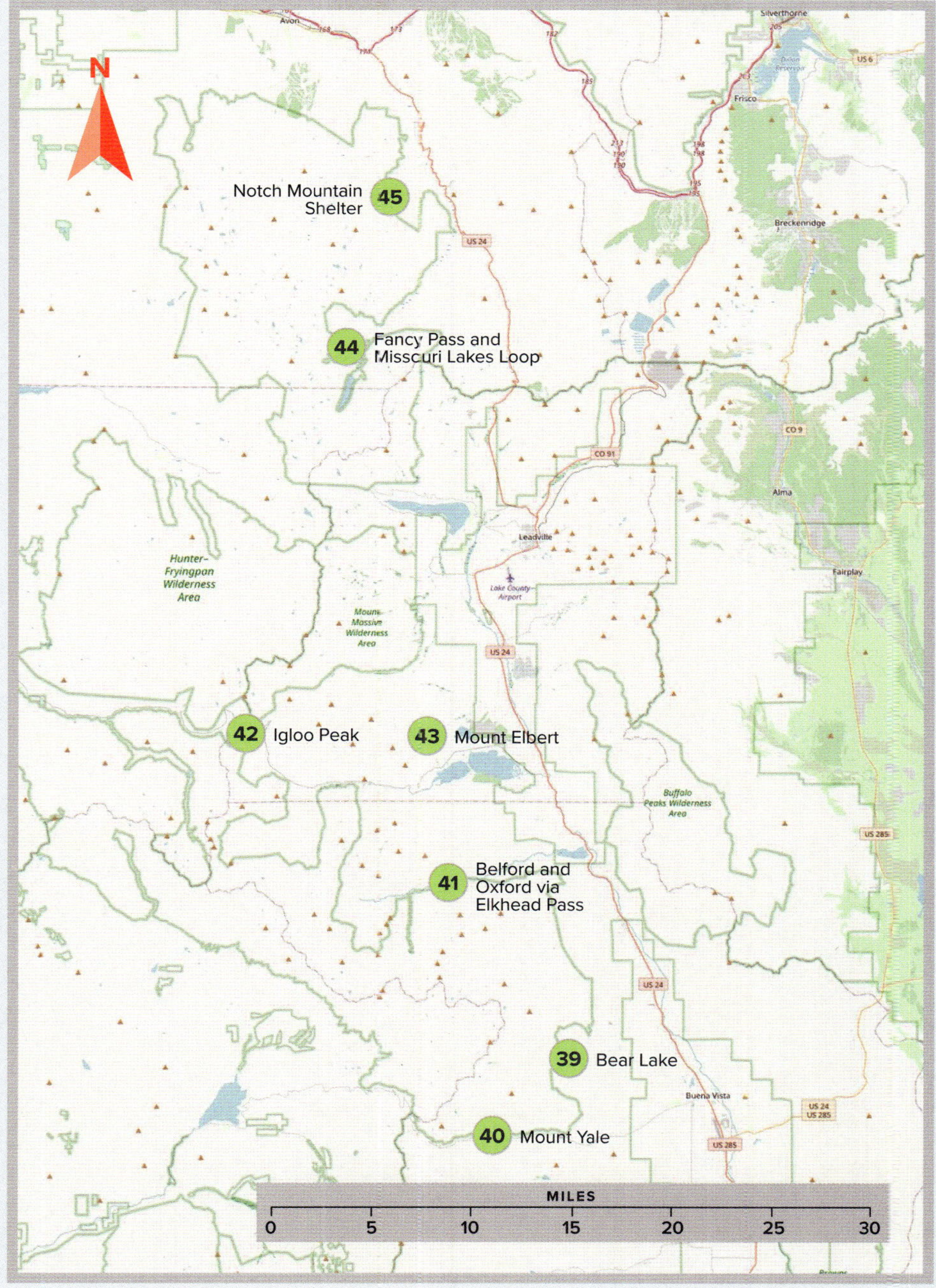

BEAR LAKE

39

Total Distance	10.7 miles (out-and-back)
Starting Elevation	9,450 feet
High Point Elevation	12,410 feet
Total Elevation Gain	2,700 feet
Difficulty	■ Intermediate
Round-trip Time	2–3 hours
Runability	95%
Nearest Town	Buena Vista

COMMENT: At 12,410 feet, Bear Lake is still dwarfed by nearby peaks. This route travels along quite gentle terrain, allowing for a quick pace relative to the mileage. Runners pass through a variety of climate zones on the way to this high alpine lake nestled in the North Cottonwood Creek valley.

Bear Lake as viewed from the Mount Harvard Trail

When you reach tree line, glance back down the North Cottonwood Creek basin.

GETTING THERE: From Buena Vista, take CO Highway 306 2.5 miles west, then turn right (north) onto CR 361 for another 2.5 miles. Turn left (west) again onto CR 365. From here, 4WD and 8+ inches of clearance are essential. Follow 5.1 more miles to the North Cottonwood Creek Trailhead (also the trailhead for Mount Harvard and Mount Columbia).

THE ROUTE: From the North Cottonwood Creek parking area, head due west onto the broad, well-maintained Horn Fork Basin Trail past the signage. Horn Fork is the only trail at the signed trailhead. After some brief initial rolls, this gentle trail parallels the south side of North Cottonwood Creek for 1.6 miles. With just 520 feet of vertical gain in this stretch of open, mostly coniferous forest, you will likely be able to cover these early miles quickly.

Just after crossing the creek, stay right at the trail fork to head north into the Horn Fork Basin. Expect to gain more elevation over the next 2 miles. By the next trail fork at 3.6 miles, you'll be at 11,490 feet and quickly approaching tree line. At this fork, stay left on the Horn Fork Basin Trail; the right-hand trail ascends the southwest rib of 14er Mount Columbia. Continue north at a steady pace as you transition from tree line into willows and wildflowers. In high summer, the surrounding meadows are full of columbines and Indian paintbrush, particularly where the trail draws close to the creek. The high ridgeline between Mount Harvard and Mount Columbia looms ahead.

Switchbacks and a turn back westward remain in the final 1.8 miles. While this is steeper than the beginning of the route, this is still a mellow slope grade (average of 10 degrees). You should feel quite comfortable holding a jogging pace here.

The last trail fork, a left, comes at 12,360 feet and 5.1 miles, just 0.3 mile and 50 vertical feet from Bear Lake. The lake is nestled close beneath the western edge of Horn Fork Basin. Imposing Mount Harvard, at 14,420 feet the third highest peak in the state, looms directly to your northwest. Take a few moments to breathe and have a quick snack before retracing your steps for an exhilarating descent back along the creeks to the trailhead.

Mount Harvard can be added on from this point, should you want to add 1,965 vertical feet and 2.8 total miles to your excursion. However, despite the remaining 1.4 miles to Harvard's summit being almost entirely on well-maintained trail, that additional distance is steep enough that very few will be able to run that remaining ascent.

Bear Lake and the upper section of the route as viewed from the shoulder of Mount Columbia

BEAR LAKE

N
Mount Harvard
14000
Mount Columbia
Bear Lake
Peak 13560
Peak 12776
Gunnison County
Chaffee County
Trailhead
San Isabel National Forest
1.6mi
1.3mi
1.5mi
1.6mi
1.7mi
0.9mi
1.2mi
0.7mi
0.9mi
1.4mi
1.1mi
1.5mi
MILES
0   0.5   1   1.5   2

MOUNT YALE

40

Total Distance	9.5 miles (out-and-back)
Starting Elevation	9,935 feet
High Point Elevation	14,196 feet
Total Elevation Gain	4,330 feet
Difficulty	◆ Difficult
Round-trip Time	2.5–3.5 hours
Runability	70%
Nearest Town	Buena Vista
Add-on	Hartenstein Lake

COMMENT: Mount Yale is the most easily accessible 14,000-foot peak from Buena Vista. It offers a beautiful variety of terrain and scenery on the route, from broad forest trail to alpine meadow single-track to the exciting and narrow summit ridge.

GETTING THERE: Drive west out of Buena Vista on CO Highway 306. After 12.1 miles, reach the roadside 2WD, paved Denny Creek parking lot on your right. Park and locate the trailhead sign halfway up the lot.

Above tree line, there is a brief reprieve before the final 1,000-foot push to the summit ridge.

Shortly above tree line, look west across the Sawatch. The Elk Range decorates the horizon.

THE ROUTE: The first mile of the Denny Creek Trail is reminiscent of popular East Coast trails. The 6-foot-wide trail through coniferous forest offers plenty of room for all pedestrians. These initial pitches are best suited to a power hike as you warm up. By the time you reach the signed trail fork at 1.3 miles, the trail has grown narrower, softer, and more shaded. Turn right to continue up the Mount Yale trail.

This section crosses and parallels the unnamed northern tributary of Denny Creek for 1.3 miles, passing many wildflower meadows and backcountry camping spots. At 2.2 miles, the trail turns steeply upward to gain 800 feet to tree line over the next 0.8 mile. In this stretch, 12,000- and 13,000-foot peaks begin to peek through the trees to your south.

Upon exiting tree line into the broad, meadowed southern shoulder of Mount Yale, you will be able to see 14ers Mount Princeton and Mount Antero to the south, two distinct points on the rocky ridgelines. Your route continues to meander northeast toward the summit, alternating between relatively mellow sections of single-track and rock-stepped switchbacks for 0.8 mile. This section of the trail is particularly picturesque amid the high alpine meadow spotted with erratic boulders, and with views of both the adjacent valleys and peaks.

At 13,190 feet and mile 3.7, switch to a steady power hike for the hardest section of the route: 855 feet of vertical gain in 0.4 mile. These rocky alpine switchbacks are

From the shoulder of Mount Yale, look south at Mount Princeton, Mount Antero, and many 13ers.

the loosest section of trail, and the elevation gain will have your lungs and glutes working hard. But relief awaits at 13,960 feet, as you reach the dip in the summit ridge from which the trail becomes considerably less steep. Pause for snacks, water, a wind layer, and a few photos.

The final 0.3 mile eastward is relatively gradual but is the most exposed and technical section of the route. While it is only Class 2, it is narrow and requires attention. Some runners may prefer to use their hands for stability along the rocky summit ridge. Reach the summit at 4.5 miles and 14,196 feet. This high point is the heart of the Sawatch 14ers, so the surrounding views here are particularly recognizable.

On the descent, high feet are absolutely essential for this technical trail run. You can pick up speed on the broad shoulder from 13,190 down to tree line at 11,900 and during the final 1.3 miles back to the trailhead. Those wishing to add another 3.4 miles to their day can turn right at the trail fork and head west to Hartenstein Lake at 11,600 feet.

MOUNT YALE

Mt Yale Trail
Mount Yale-South Peak
Mount Yale
San Isabel National Forest
FR 306
CR 306
Collegiate Peaks Wilderness Area
San Isabel National Forest
Trailhead
MILES
Peak 12955
Peak 12956
Denny Creek
Hartenstein Lake
Peak 12739
Turner Peak
CR 306
CR 346
0.4mi
2.7mi
1.3mi
1.7mi
1.0mi
N

BELFORD AND OXFORD VIA ELKHEAD PASS

41

Total Distance	11 miles (out-and-back)
Starting Elevation	9,650 feet
High Point Elevation	14,197 feet
Total Elevation Gain	5,800 feet
Difficulty	◆ Difficult
Round-trip Time	3.5–5 hours
Runability	75%
Nearest Towns	Buena Vista/Twin Lakes

COMMENT: These two Collegiate Peaks are a high-altitude double hitter of good running terrain. Located in the central Sawatch, they pack a punch of vertical gain and offer stellar 360-degree views, with especially breathtaking perspectives of Mount Harvard.

GETTING THERE: Turn west off of US Highway 24 at CR 390 between Granite and Buena Vista. Stay straight on CR 390 for 7.5 miles. The road becomes rougher after you pass the split with CR 397 (keep right), but it is still manageable with low clear-

View from the summit of nearby Missouri Mountain, looking south across the Sawatch Range

At 5.7 miles, look back along the ridge from Elkhead Pass before traversing over to Oxford Peak.

ance if you take your time. From that fork, you have 3.3 of the 7.5 miles remaining to the Missouri Gulch Trailhead parking lot. Mountain bikers can reach this lot, and there are sections of fence where it is possible to lock a bike.

THE ROUTE: The first 2 miles up into Missouri Gulch have changed slightly following the historic avalanches in 2018, one of which took down a massive swatch of the mixed conifer and aspen forest between the trailhead and upper Missouri Gulch.

After the first mile of switchbacks and contouring toward the valley, emerge into broad switchbacks through the sapling regrowth of what was demolished in the avalanches. This section of the route can be especially gorgeous in mid- to late September, offering glimpses of golden and fiery orange aspen stands on nearby mountainsides while you ascend the gold-dappled trail. You will pass several cabin frames from old mining claims as you meander generally southward.

At 2 miles and 11,500 feet, emerge from the last full grove of conifers into dense willows. Belford's northwest ridge and the north face of Missouri Mountain are now directly in view as you make your way farther into the basin. Reach a fork among a few particularly tenacious conifers at 2.3 miles. Rather than taking the left up Belford's ridge (signed for Mount Belford), continue south as Missouri Mountain looms higher and higher overhead. The next trail fork, between Missouri Mountain on the right and Elkhead Pass, is a better left turn at 3.9 miles. Follow

Missouri Mountain looms to the south 3 miles into the route. Soon you'll turn east toward Elkhead Pass.

this trail southeast toward Elkhead Pass, which will offer your first glimpse across Pine Creek Basin at the northwest face of Mount Harvard.

From this 13,220-foot saddle, turn left again to continue up the slopes of Mount Belford rather than descending from Elkhead Pass into the Pine Creek Basin. Wend your way northeast and then north up the gentle slopes. The fourth fork of your journey, which is not signed, comes at 5.6 miles and 14,028 feet. Although the summit of Mount Belford is only 0.3 mile away, I recommend delaying your gratification and instead turning right to travel the 1.2 miles to Mount Oxford. This connecting trail is idyllic trail running for such a high elevation, with a quick descent to the 13,520 saddle and then a gentle 610-foot climb to Oxford's summit.

From there, retrace your steps. You may want to power hike the steep reascent to Belford's ridge, but once you've regained it, your second summit is mere minutes away. Now you have a choice: you can descend the gentle slopes of Elkhead Pass to the south, or if you have strong quads and sturdy knees, you can race down the switchbacks of Belford's northwest ridge for a new perspective.

These options are roughly time equivalent as your momentum carries you back down Missouri Gulch to the trailhead. Running down Belford's northwest ridge will take you back to the trail fork you bypassed on your ascent, so it is a very straightforward right turn at the bottom of the ridge to head back to Missouri Gulch.

BELFORD AND OXFORD VIA ELKHEAD PASS

IGLOO PEAK

42

Total Distance	5.1 miles (out-and-back)
Starting Elevation	12,100 feet
High Point Elevation	13,060 feet
Total Elevation Gain	1,200 feet
Difficulty	● Beginner
Round-trip Time	1–1.5 hours
Runability	95%
Nearest Towns	Aspen/Twin Lakes
Add-on	Mountain Boy Peak (13,198 feet)

COMMENT: The 13,060-foot Igloo Peak often goes overlooked by all but passionate springtime skiers and snowboarders. This brief jaunt southwest of Independence Pass deserves more attention and love for its excellent views, summertime accessibility, and suitability as a warm-up or introductory alpine run.

Grizzly Peak A due south from Igloo's summit

GETTING THERE: From Aspen, head east on CO Highway 82 for 19 miles; from Twin Lakes, head west on CO 82 for 17.5 miles. Park in the Independence Pass viewing deck lot. There is a short walkway at the top of the pass where visitors can stroll south to a viewing deck. Note that dogs are allowed on leash, but unless your dog is agile enough to scramble up several 6-foot stretches of rock at the end of the route, it is not recommended to bring them.

THE ROUTE: The trail for Igloo Peak turns right (west) from the main viewpoint path just 0.1 mile from the parking lot and wends along the wide, mellow ridgeline extending southward. It is not signed. This single-track takes runners through 2.5 miles of high alpine meadows, as well as over Peak 12,812'. The trail is thin but clear; be mindful to stay on the trail to avoid creating new foot impact on the alpine tundra.

This route has the added aesthetic of cliffs dropping away on the eastern side; in snowy season, these are entries to long-lasting snow bowls popular among backcountry skiers. To the west, the Elk Range ripples along the horizon. To the south, east, and north, some of the more dramatic Sawatch views unfold, from dramatic low 13ers to a collection of the highest peaks in Colorado.

As the trail climbs, the ridgeline grows more narrow and dramatic. The last 0.1 mile to the summit involves some mild scrambling. It is brief Class 2+ and may pass

12,000- and 13,000-foot peaks to the southwest

quickly for those moving fast. This section is likely to be exhilarating for runners who enjoy technical challenges. It could, however, present difficulties with canine companions. Past this short stretch of scrambling, the remaining distance to the summit is on wide, easy, musical talus trail. After enjoying a well-deserved rest at the summit, remember to exercise caution on the descent, particularly in those upper talusy and scrambly portions.

If you want to add on Mountain Boy Peak, follow the ridgeline east from the summit of Igloo Peak and lose 250 vertical feet in 0.1 mile to the saddle. From this low point, continue to follow the thin footpath and gain 400 vertical feet over the next 0.4 mile. While this section does not exceed Class 2, the initial descent from Igloo to the saddle does have exposure, and this descent and ascent are by far the steepest grades on this run. The broad summit of Mountain Boy Peak offers similar views but with the added dramatics of looking down Mountain Boy's sharp eastern ridge. Recharge your legs, then turn westward to retrace your steps.

IGLOO PEAK

N
12400
12400
11400
12000
Hunter-Fryingpan Wilderness Area
11200
11400
11600
11800
11000 Collegiate Peaks Wilderness Area
White River National Forest
11400
Independence Creek
12400
12000
11800
12200
12400
12000
Pitkin County
Pitkin County
Peak 12812
Lake County
Peak 13041
12200
11400
11600
11800
12400
Grizzly Lake
11600
12400
12000
3.5mi
CO 82
12000
Trailhead
Independence Pass
Lake County
12600
12400
12200
11800
11400
11600
11800
12000
12400
12000
11600
11800
12000
12400
Mountain Boy Peak
12800
13000
12200
11800
12000
11600
11400
San Isabel National Forest
0.8mi
Lake County
12600
12400
12200
12200
4.2mi
MILES
0   0.5   1   1.5

MOUNT ELBERT

43

Total Distance	10.7 miles (out-and-back)
Starting Elevation	10,510 feet
High Point Elevation	14,433 feet
Total Elevation Gain	4,080 feet
Difficulty	◆ Difficult (Note: Elbert is rated as Difficult not because of trail difficulty, mileage, or exposure, but simply because it tops out at such a high elevation.)
Round-trip Time	3.5–5 hours
Runability	75%
Nearest Towns	Aspen/Twin Lakes/Leadville

COMMENT: At 14,433 feet, Mount Elbert is the highest peak in Colorado and the second highest peak in the contiguous 48 states. Given its proximity to Leadville, it is a popular training ground for high-elevation trail runners. This east ridge route is a picturesque alternative to the standard northeast ridge.

The well-marked turn from the Colorado Trail to start heading up the East Ridge Trail

Left: A view north to Mount Massive from the shoulder of the ridge around 12,500 feet
Right: On the descent, enjoy quick rolling terrain through aspen.

GETTING THERE: From US Highway 24, turn west at the exit to Twin Lakes. Drive 4 miles on CO Highway 82 to a turn northwest onto CR 24. Follow it 1.3 miles to the South Elbert 2WD, paved parking lot. From Twin Lakes, it is 2.4 miles to CR 24. Vehicles with 2WD or 4WD and with less than 9 inches of clearance should park here at the lower South Mount Elbert Trailhead. This will add 1.7 miles and 908 feet of vertical gain via the dirt road or 2.3 miles and 985 vertical gain via the CT/CDT connecting trail. If you have a high-clearance 4WD vehicle, continue 1.8 miles on Forest Road 125B to the upper South Mount Elbert Trailhead at 10,510 feet.

THE ROUTE: From the upper trailhead's small dirt parking lot and first set of trailhead signs, follow the blocked-off section of road 0.2 mile to a second set of trailhead signs at the intersection with the Colorado Trail. Turn right (north) and cross a wooden bridge. Follow the rolling trail north through aspen forest to a signed fork at 0.4 mile. Here, take a left onto the South Mount Elbert East Ridge Trail and begin ascending well-maintained, gentle switchbacks through aspen groves.

Around 11,000 feet, the forest transitions to fir and pine and the delightfully soft, spongy soil that comes with these trees. This section of trail is runnable if you are pushing for speed but is also well suited for a quick power hike for those giving a more measured effort. At 11,540 feet, the switchbacks relax. Cross through a series of wildflower meadows and conifer groves as you approach tree line.

La Plata Peak is visible to the south from switchbacks above 14,000 on the descent.

The conifer stands grow fewer and farther between as the switchbacks begin to include stone steps and corral through log fences built to protect restored sections of alpine tundra. Tree line finally terminates just below 12,000 feet (unusually high for Colorado on this broad and gentle east-facing ridge). This brief plateau offers a moment of active recovery.

From here, the trail grows more rugged. The next 1.8 miles and 1,800 vertical feet switchback up the northern edge of the ridge, with talus steps and sharp corners galore. The musical mountain breeze and pika chorus is a pleasant accompaniment to your heartbeat. At the top of this section, the trail grows friendlier and more gradual for the final 0.8 mile, meandering slightly south in gaining the final 700 vertical feet.

Less than 0.1 mile from the summit, meet the Northeast Ridge Trail as stacked rock wind shelters begin appearing. This highest summit in the state is roomy, and especially on summer weekend mornings, expect to have plenty of company while you take in the spectacular views. After putting on a wind jacket or other layer of clothing and having a snack, shake out your legs and start the invigorating descent.

MOUNT ELBERT

FANCY PASS AND MISSOURI LAKES LOOP

44

Total Distance	8.8 miles (loop)
Starting Elevation	10,090 feet
High Point Elevation	12,310 feet
Total Elevation Gain	2,770 feet
Difficulty	■ Intermediate
Round-trip Time	2.25–3.5 hours
Runability	80%
Nearest Towns	Red Cliff/Minturn

COMMENT: This route in the northern Sawatch mixes some steady climbing with forest and alpine single-track reminiscent of typical East Coast terrain. It is a good jaunt for fitting into a camping trip or taking a half-day detour on a drive to Leadville or Buena Vista from the Front Range.

Look down at Fancy Lake as you ascend eastward toward the pass.

Looking south across the Treasure Vault basin

GETTING THERE: Turn west off of US Highway 24, 2 miles south of Red Cliff onto Homestake Reservoir Road (CR 703). Follow for 7.8 miles, then take a slight right onto Missouri Creek Road (CR 704) and follow for another 2.2 miles to the Missouri Lakes and Fancy Pass Trailheads. These two parking areas are roughly 0.25 mile apart. Because these are popular trailheads, an earlier start will allow closer parking. Vehicles with 6–7 inches of clearance and 4WD are helpful. It is possible to mountain bike to these trailheads; should you choose to do so, be aware that you're likely to encounter heavy car traffic. There are no bike racks, so bikes must be locked to trees or the trail signs.

THE ROUTE: Start up the Fancy Pass Trail, which heads roughly westward while switchbacking through dense, old-growth coniferous forest. Glacial erratic boulders and lichen-draped branches and logs abound. After 0.9 mile, reach a cut-log creek crossing. From here, the forest grows less thick and more boreal as you continue to gain elevation. At 1.1 miles, ascend through the first of several tiered meadows. The trail parallels a narrow water-cut gorge for a stretch in between some of these clearings.

Starting at mile 2.3, ascend steeply and start watching the trail closely. At the top of this set of switchbacks, there are many impacted campsites for Fancy Lake, and it can be easy to lose the main trail for an offshoot, as there aren't signs among

Prepare for your long descent past the Missouri Lakes beneath Savage Peak.

the dispersed camping spots. Navigate due north through these campsites to intersect the clear and signed Fancy Lakes Trail, and take a left. You are fast approaching tree line, and the summit of Fancy Pass is now just 0.6 mile away. This stretch is steep and rocky, ascending 800 feet in this short distance. Most will want to settle into a power hike to the crest of the pass, a portal into a high-alpine basin.

Keep high feet as you descend past wildflowers and pika. This interlude of downhill and flat lasts only 1.1 miles. Shortly after you turn left at the signed Treasure Vault trail junction and pass Treasure Vault Lake, start ascending southward toward the pass to Missouri Lakes. This second high point, at 4.6 miles and 11,995 feet, marks the end of the climbing. Now comes an exhilarating descent passing lake after lake. These bodies of water aren't the only stunning views. Savage Peak, 13,139 feet high, looms on the south rim of the valley, dominating photos.

Once you've passed the last of the Missouri Lakes around 5.8 miles, 3 miles remain of the loop, and the next 2-mile stretch remains technical. Light feet are essential as you follow Missouri Creek east. At 7.9 miles, the trail broadens into old road, and less than a mile northbound remains to close the loop. The relatively flat terrain is ideal for a swift finish through the conifer forest.

FANCY PASS AND MISSOURI LAKES LOOP

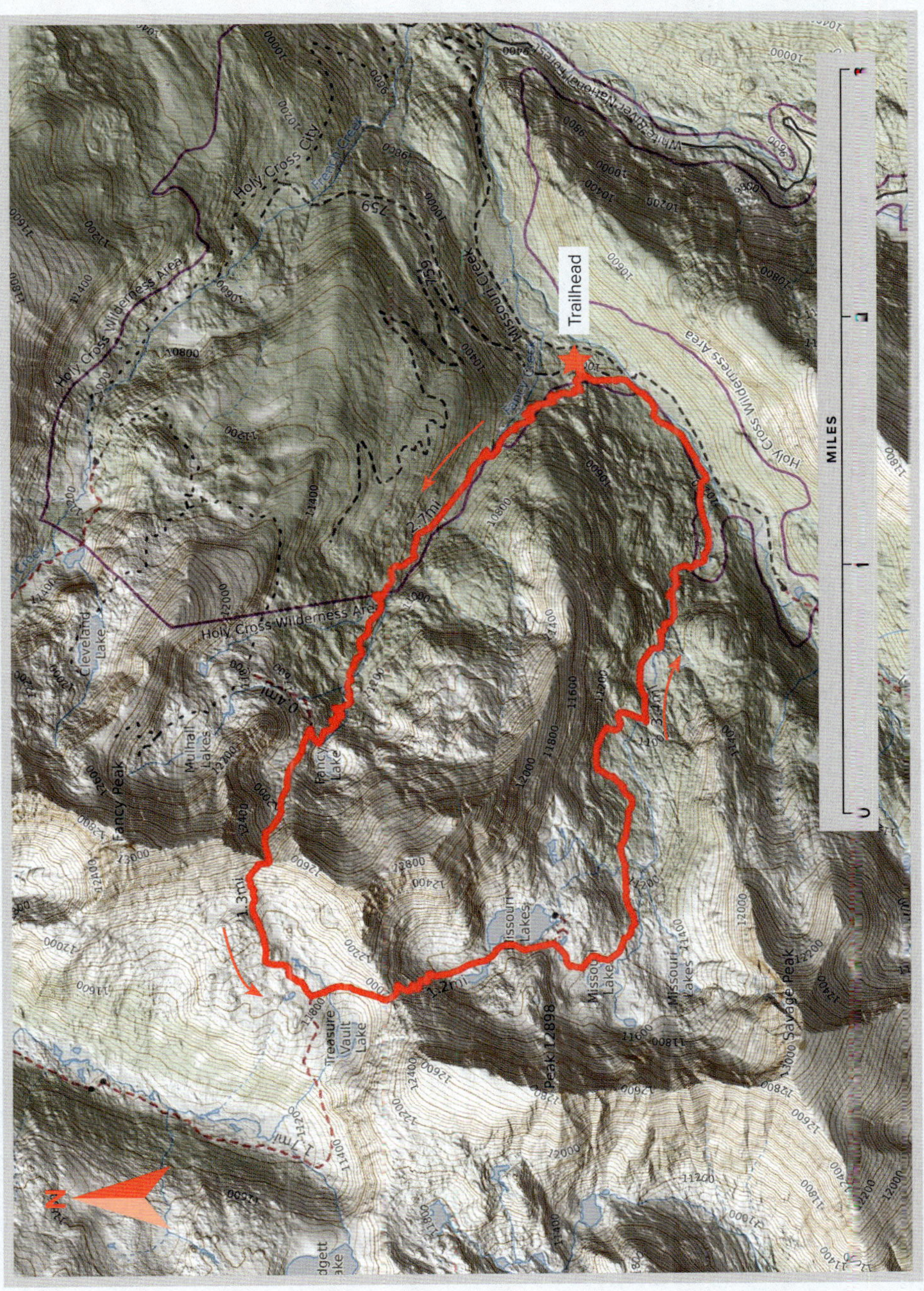

NOTCH MOUNTAIN SHELTER

45

Total Distance	10.4 miles (out-and-back)
Starting Elevation	10,380 feet
High Point Elevation	13,095 feet
Total Elevation Gain	2,800 feet
Difficulty	◆ Difficult
Round-trip Time	2–4 hours
Runability	85%
Nearest Town	Minturn

COMMENT: Notch Mountain Shelter sits at a broad, flat point on the eastern shoulder of the half-moon Halo Ridge massif. The shelter looks west at the stark prominence of Mount of the Holy Cross, while lower ridgelines unfurl to the east and north. The grade of the trail is gradual, but the overall vert and the upper stretches of the route provide a robust challenge. This is a great route for testing out the legs after checking off some of the introductory alpine runs.

Looking back along the trail to the north before starting the switchbacks

Mount of the Holy Cross dominates the western horizon.

GETTING THERE: Drive south on US Highway 24 from Minturn for 3 miles to Notch Mountain/Tigiwon Road. Turn right (west) onto this dirt road. While the next mile is well-graded, 4WD and at least 7 inches of clearance are essential. From the turn off of US 24, continue 4.4 miles. When you reach a fork, turn right again to stay on Notch Mountain/Tigiwon Road and follow for an additional 3.9 miles to the Half Moon and Fall Creek Trailheads.

THE ROUTE: Start up the Fall Creek Trail. The first 2.1 miles in the forest are gradual and very runnable, gaining only 400 feet per mile on soft, needle-padded trail. Pass through the high, widely spaced pine trees and gradually start ascending, traversing south along the eastern slopes of Notch Mountain. At 2.3 miles, reach the signed trail juncture in a clearing and turn right (west) onto the Notch Mountain Trail.

The next 0.4 mile consists of steep, varied switchbacks through coniferous forest. You are approaching tree line, so the stands of trees are becoming

Turn right off the Fall Creek Trail onto the Notch Mountain Trail to start the bulk of the ascent.

As the ridge flattens and the trail becomes faint, Notch Mountain Shelter comes into view, with part of the Halo Ridge looming behind it.

fewer and farther between. After gaining 300 feet, the slope relaxes somewhat as the trail heads south across a wide alpine meadow. In midsummer, the wildflowers in the next 1.2 miles are decadent. This stretch of terrain is very runnable and excellent for photos. Toward the top of this mellow section, tree line peters out.

Now above 12,000 feet, the next set of switchbacks are more technical and rocky than those you've encountered so far. Pace yourself: you have 850 feet and 1.3 miles remaining to your objective, all of which is on these relentless talus switchbacks.

The lower section of the descent through the trees goes quickly.

Occupy your mind by taking in the excellent views to the south and east. Soon enough, the top of the ridge will start to creep into view, until you turn a corner and discover Mount of the Holy Cross peeping onto your western foreground.

Pause in the shade of the old stone shelter at the end of the maintained trail to take in the iconic 14,005-foot peak, eat a snack, and drink some water. Then shake out your limbs and race down the switchbacks with high, quick feet. This 5-mile descent is truly thrilling, optimal for accessing a joyful flow-state of childlike fun along these east-facing slopes.

NOTCH MOUNTAIN SHELTER

Cathedral Lake as viewed
from the top of Electric Pass Peak

ACKNOWLEDGMENTS

A guidebook is not a one-person endeavor. A vast team of people gave time, thought, and energy to this publication, and I am extremely grateful to everyone who has been involved in various parts of the process. I am deeply thankful to Jeff Golden, my friend who first demonstrated belief in the concept and laid the groundwork for this book to come into existence. I would like to thank the Colorado Mountain Club Press, particularly editors Sarah Gorecki and Casey Blaine, for the hours they have put into guiding my words to their best form and for publishing this guidebook.

Thank you to the friends who have contributed photos, route insights, and brainstorming: Madeline Fones, Robin Lindsay, Kate West, Nathan Boyer-Rechlin, Will Fisher, Tony Vazquez, Jeff Richards, and others. Of these, particular thanks go to Madeline Fones for my favorite photo I've ever seen from the Four Pass Loop (p. iii), and to Kate West for agreeing to run Grays and Torreys with me at dusk on the summer solstice several years ago. I'm also grateful to the English teachers and mentors I've had in my life, especially Andy Popinchalk for his unwavering faith in my writing and outdoor pursuits, and Bob Cowser for showing me that alignment of passions is the best starting point for a project. Any inconsistencies or omissions are my own, borne of the same creative impulse that leads to off-trail exploration.

I deeply appreciate the large mountain community throughout Colorado, especially the many groups and individuals that volunteer time, labor, and donations to protect the wild spaces we enjoy and maintain the countless trail systems in the Colorado high country. I am in awe of the athletes, both professional and recreational, who have blazed the trail of mountain running and skyrunning. I am grateful both for the inspiration they provide to so many of us and for the opportunity to contribute a small piece to the pursuit of this athletic niche.

		MILEAGE	DIFFICULTY	VERTICAL GAIN	NOTES
5	Mount Sniktau	3.8 mi.	● Beginner	1,800'	
14	Midway Tarn	4.5 mi.	● Beginner	1,502'	
24	Highland Mary Lakes	5 mi.	● Beginner	1,340'	
42	Igloo Peak	5.1 mi.	● Beginner	1,200'	
25	Columbine Lake	5.7 mi.	■ Intermediate	2,625'	
6	Mount Flora	6.2 mi.	■ Intermediate	2,275'	
12	Mount Sherman and Mount Sheridan	6.5 mi.	■ Intermediate	2,750'	
26	Matterhorn Creek	6.7 mi.	● Beginner	2,465'	
31	Lily Lake	6.8 mi.	● Beginner	1,700'	
2	Blue Lake and Mitchell Lake	7 mi.	● Beginner	1,190'	
10	Quandary Peak	7 mi.	■ Intermediate	3,450'	
32	Music Pass	7.2 mi.	● Beginner	2,090'	
7	Mount Bierstadt	7.5 mi.	■ Intermediate	2,775'	
11	Decalibron Loop	7.5 mi.	■ Intermediate	3,400'	
1	Chasm Lake	8 mi.	■ Intermediate	2,500'	
27	Handies Peak	8.2 mi.	■ Intermediate	3,650'	
23	Blue Lakes Basin	8.4 mi.	■ Intermediate	2,900'	
3	Old Baldy	8.5 mi.	■ Intermediate	2,880'	
8	Grays and Torreys Peaks	8.5 mi.	■ Intermediate	3,650'	
15	Lost Man Loop	8.8 mi.	■ Intermediate	1,610'	
44	Fancy Pass and Missouri Lakes Loop	8.8 mi.	■ Intermediate	2,770'	
29	Redcloud Peak	9 mi.	■ Intermediate	3,700'	
40	Mount Yale	9.5 mi.	◆ Difficult	4,330'	
37	Zapata Lake	9.6 mi.	■ Intermediate	3,300'	
38	Willow Lake	9.6 mi.	■ Intermediate	3,500'	
35	Humboldt Peak	9.8 mi.	◆ Difficult	4,200'	
28	Cooper Lake	10 mi.	■ Intermediate	2,380'	
33	Lake of the Clouds	10.2 mi.	■ Intermediate	2,190'	
45	Notch Mountain Shelter	10.4 mi.	◆ Difficult	2,800'	
39	Bear Lake	10.7 mi.	■ Intermediate	2,700'	
43	Mount Elbert	10.7 mi.	◆ Difficult	4,080'	
16	Aspen Highlands	11 mi.	◆ Difficult	4,760'	
41	Belford and Oxford via Elkhead Pass	11 mi.	◆ Difficult	5,800'	
18	Electric Pass Peak and Leahy Peak	12 mi.	■ Intermediate	4,100'	
17	Capitol Lake	12.6 mi.	■ Intermediate	2,600'	
34	Phantom Terrace Loop	12.6 mi.	◆ Difficult	4,400'	
36	Obstruction Peak	12.8 mi.	◆◆ Most Difficult	4,700'	
19	Castle Peak	13.5 mi.	◆◆ Most Difficult	4,600'	
20	Mount Sopris	13.5 mi.	◆◆ Most Difficult	4,665'	
13	Tenmile Traverse	14.7 mi.	◆◆ Most Difficult	8,320'	
4	High Lonesome Loop	15.7 mi.	◆ Difficult	3,560'	
21	Snowmass Three Pass Loop	23 mi.	◆◆ Most Difficult	5,930'	
30	The Window	24.8 mi.	◆◆ Most Difficult	4,900'	
9	Pikes Peak	25.1 mi.	◆◆ Most Difficult	7,545'	
22	Four Pass Loop	28 mi.	◆◆ Most Difficult	7,265'	

CHECKLIST OF RUNS BY VERTICAL GAIN

		MILEAGE	DIFFICULTY	VERTICAL GAIN	NOTES
2	**Blue Lake and Mitchell Lake**	7 mi.	● Beginner	1,190'	
42	**Igloo Peak**	5.1 mi.	● Beginner	1,200'	
24	**Highland Mary Lakes**	5 mi.	● Beginner	1,340'	
14	**Midway Tarn**	4.5 mi.	● Beginner	1,502'	
15	**Lost Man Loop**	8.8 mi.	■ Intermediate	1,610'	
31	**Lily Lake**	6.8 mi.	● Beginner	1,700'	
5	**Mount Sniktau**	3.8 mi.	● Beginner	1,800'	
32	**Music Pass**	7.2 mi.	● Beginner	2,090'	
33	**Lake of the Clouds**	10.2 mi.	■ Intermediate	2,190'	
6	**Mount Flora**	6.2 mi.	■ Intermediate	2,275'	
28	**Cooper Lake**	10 mi.	■ Intermediate	2,380'	
26	**Matterhorn Creek**	6.7 mi.	● Beginner	2,465'	
1	**Chasm Lake**	8 mi.	■ Intermediate	2,500'	
17	**Capitol Lake**	12.6 mi.	■ Intermediate	2,600'	
25	**Columbine Lake**	5.7 mi.	■ Intermediate	2,625'	
39	**Bear Lake**	10.7 mi.	■ Intermediate	2,700'	
12	**Mount Sherman and Mount Sheridan**	6.5 mi.	■ Intermediate	2,750'	
44	**Fancy Pass and Missouri Lakes Loop**	8.8 mi.	■ Intermediate	2,770'	
7	**Mount Bierstadt**	7.5 mi.	■ Intermediate	2,775'	
45	**Notch Mountain Shelter**	10.4 mi.	◆ Difficult	2,800'	
3	**Old Baldy**	8.5 mi.	■ Intermediate	2,880'	
23	**Blue Lakes Basin**	8.4 mi.	■ Intermediate	2,900'	
37	**Zapata Lake**	9.6 mi.	■ Intermediate	3,300'	
11	**Decalibron Loop**	7.5 mi.	■ Intermediate	3,400'	
10	**Quandary Peak**	7 mi.	■ Intermediate	3,450'	
38	**Willow Lake**	9.6 mi.	■ Intermediate	3,500'	
4	**High Lonesome Loop**	15.7 mi.	◆ Difficult	3,560'	
8	**Grays and Torreys Peaks**	8.5 mi.	■ Intermediate	3,650'	
27	**Handies Peak**	8.2 mi.	■ Intermediate	3,650'	
29	**Redcloud Peak**	9 mi.	■ Intermediate	3,700'	
43	**Mount Elbert**	10.7 mi.	◆ Difficult	4,080'	
18	**Electric Pass Peak and Leahy Peak**	12 mi.	■ Intermediate	4,100'	
35	**Humboldt Peak**	9.8 mi.	◆ Difficult	4,200'	
40	**Mount Yale**	9.5 mi.	◆ Difficult	4,330'	
34	**Phantom Terrace Loop**	12.6 mi.	◆ Difficult	4,400'	
19	**Castle Peak**	13.5 mi.	◆◆ Most Difficult	4,600'	
36	**Obstruction Peak**	12.8 mi.	◆◆ Most Difficult	4,700'	
20	**Mount Sopris**	13.5 mi.	◆◆ Most Difficult	4,665'	
16	**Aspen Highlands**	11 mi.	◆ Difficult	4,760'	
30	**The Window**	24.8 mi.	◆◆ Most Difficult	4,900'	
41	**Belford and Oxford via Elkhead Pass**	11 mi.	◆ Difficult	5,800'	
21	**Snowmass Three Pass Loop**	23 mi.	◆◆ Most Difficult	5,930'	
22	**Four Pass Loop**	28 mi.	◆◆ Most Difficult	7,265'	
9	**Pikes Peak**	25.1 mi.	◆◆ Most Difficult	7,545'	
13	**Tenmile Traverse**	14.7 mi.	◆◆ Most Difficult	8,320'	

ABOUT THE AUTHOR

Annalise Grueter has been exploring Colorado trails her entire life. She started hiking and backpacking as a child and running at the age of 11. She ran her first Colorado peak at the age of 15 (Electric Pass Peak), and steadily fell in love with exploring mountains and high places on foot. A graduate of National Outdoor Leadership School (NOLS), she has taught and mentored both children and adults on camping, orienteering, and safe mountain practices.

Annalise is a marathoner and ultramarathoner as well as an avid hiker. She has made over 154 summits of Colorado's 14ers and reached the summits of the highest peaks in California, Washington, Mexico, Germany, and Tanzania. She enjoys exploring mountain ranges around the world, especially through sports such as mountain running and ski mountaineering.

The author standing on 13er Leahy Peak during a run.

Recreate with RIMS

Give back to the land you love with the CMC RIMS (Recreation Impact Monitoring System) mobile app: If you spot a downed tree, trail erosion, trash, or poor signage while you're exploring the places in this book, open the app and submit a quick report so that land managers can address the issue. Learn more and get started at cmc.org/RIMS.

cmc.org/RIMS

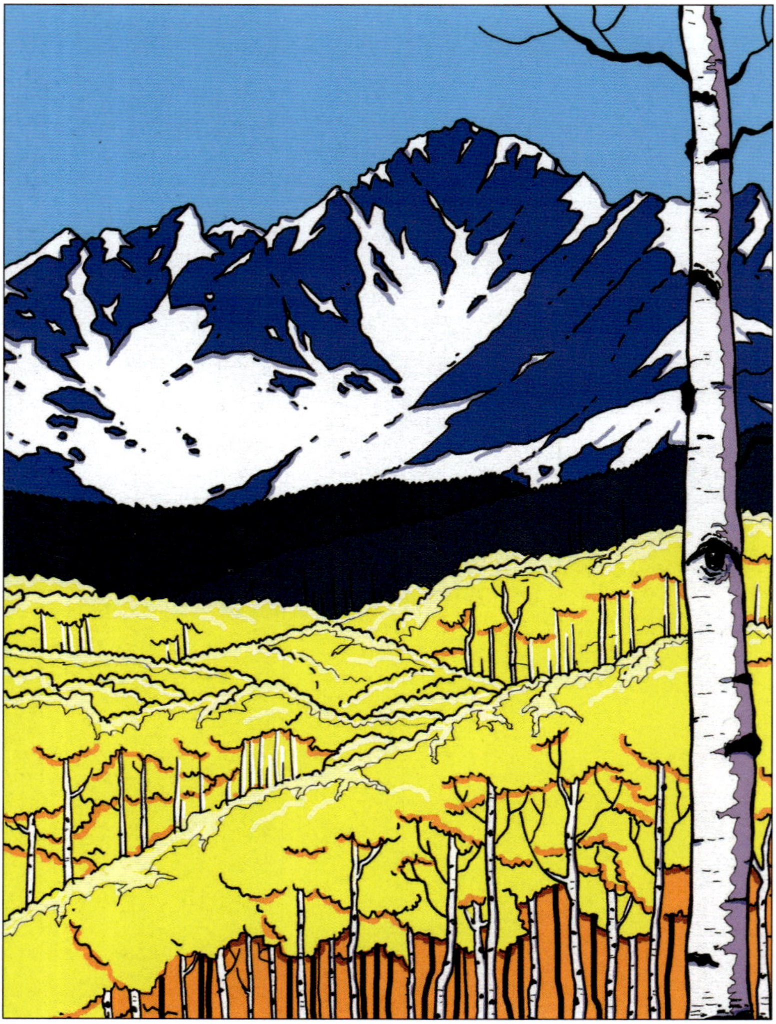